THE HISTORY OF THE SUNBEAM ALPINE

JOHN WILLSHIRE

AMBERLEY

Cover image: Tony Barron with co-driver Dominic Barron in a Sunbeam Harrington Le Mans, competing in the 1995 Monte Carlo Challenge. (Tony Barron Collection)

First published 2015

Amberley Publishing
The Hill, Stroud,
Gloucestershire, GL5 4EP

www.amberley-books.com

Copyright © John Willshire, 2015

The right of John Willshire to be identified as the Author
of this work has been asserted in accordance with the
Copyrights, Designs and Patents Act 1988.

All rights reserved. No part of this book may be reprinted
or reproduced or utilised in any form or by any electronic,
mechanical or other means, now known or hereafter invented,
including photocopying and recording, or in any information
storage or retrieval system, without the permission in writing
from the Publishers.

ISBN 978 1 4456 4758 6 (print)
ISBN 978 1 4456 4759 3 (ebook)

British Library Cataloguing in Publication Data.
A catalogue record for this book is available from the British Library.

Typeset in 10pt on 13pt Celeste.
Typesetting by Amberley Publishing.
Printed in the UK.

Contents

Foreword	4
Design and Development	5
Production	13
Hybrids	26
International Rallying	32
International Racing	45
Club Racing	66
Ownership	82
Bibliography	96

Foreword

There have been many books written about the Rootes Group and the cars they have produced, so when John invited me to write a forward to his book I was intrigued to see how yet another book would tell the story.

So often, filling a book with statistics can be very boring for the reader, and I have several books of that kind in my collection. However, although John's book is full of statistics it is written in such a way as to flow and keep the reader interested and credit is due for the obvious research which he has carried out.

My interest was tilted towards the racing and rallying side of the book, and John has covered this in great detail.

I well remember the tests carried out at both Silverstone and Lindley covered here. Norman Garrad told Peter Harper and I that if we could test the cars without any problems we would be racing at Sebring and Le Mans. We made sure we did not break the cars. With the bankings at Lindley we were able to record a very high average speed without stressing the car. This impressed the Rootes family, and so the deal was done. In fact we could have driven a Reliant Robin nearly as quickly.

The collection of photos that John has included adds to the story and I feel sure everyone will enjoy reading this book.

Peter Procter

Design and Development

The Sunbeam Alpine is one of a wide variety of vehicles that was made by the Rootes Group, which at the height of its hundred-year history was one of Britain's biggest car makers. Rootes began life in the mid-1800s as a bicycle manufacturing and repair business. It was the original founder's grandsons, William and Reginald Rootes, who were responsible for the development of car manufacturing and who ran the business in its heyday.

The two Rootes brothers were of differing character, with skills that complemented each other in the running of the business. William had a gift for salesmanship, while Reginald was a talented administrator. In 1913, at the age of 18, William was already quite an entrepreneur. He had begun to build a car sales and distribution company with the money made from selling the chickens from his egg farming business. During the First World War, William became a commissioned officer. He persuaded the Admiralty, where his brother worked, to let him set up an aero-engine repair factory, saving damaged engines from the scrap heap. When the war ended William continued to develop his motor business and Reginald left a promising career in the civil service to join his brother. The company grew rapidly. In 1920 it became the agent for General Motors in Britain and by 1924 it was the country's biggest car sales and distribution business. By 1929, with a huge network of sales and service companies overseas, it had become one of the world's largest car and truck distributors.

With demand outstripping supply and lack of control over quality, the Rootes brothers decided to go into manufacturing. In 1932 they rescued the financially struggling Humber and Hillman marques then, later, others including Sunbeam and Singer, forming the Rootes Group of companies.

Sunbeam had begun as a bicycle manufacturer in 1877 and began producing cars in 1901. By 1912 they were making vehicles of such high quality they were in direct competition with Rolls-Royce. They had also branched out into aero-engine manufacture. During the First World War they were producing motorcycles, trucks, ambulances and aircraft, but Sunbeam's greatest era was in the 1920s after they merged with Talbot-Durracq. On the race track they had great success, including victory at the 1922 Tourist Trophy, two Grand Prix wins with Sir Henry Segrave, and second place at Le Mans – beating Bentley. Segrave's Sunbeam Grand Prix car, named *Tiger*, was very successful at Brooklands and set the land-speed record at 152.33 mph in 1926. Sunbeam also built Sir Malcolm Campbell's original multi-record breaking *Blue Bird* car and the huge 1,000 bhp Sunbeam which set the land-speed record at 203.79 mph in 1927, again with Segrave. After getting into financial trouble in the 1930s during the Depression, Sunbeam-Talbot went into receivership in 1935 and was purchased by the Rootes Group.

Rootes were an early adopter of badge engineering and gradually phased out production of existing models at the newly acquired companies, replacing them with designs from Humber and Hillman that were easier to mass produce and using common chassis and engines for different models aimed at various markets. Tending to spend more on sales and showrooms than on development, Rootes products were seldom very technically advanced, but they were reasonably priced, reliable and usually value for money. Both brothers were honoured with knighthoods in recognition of their huge manufacturing efforts during the Second World War, after which they continued to develop the Hillman, Humber and Sunbeam-Talbot marques.

It was immediately after the war that the British sports car first gained a following and a certain kudos in the United States, when American servicemen that were stationed in Britain shipped home their favourite means of transport, the pre-war MG T Series Midget. MG restarted production with barely any modifications immediately after the end of the war. Catching on to the demand, they produced nearly 50,000 over a ten-year period, mainly for the American market. Their new model, the MGA, was introduced in 1955 and continued with even more overseas success, with only 6 per cent of the 101,000 cars produced staying in Britain. Not wanting to miss out on huge sales potential, Triumph and Austin Healey jumped on the bandwagon in 1953 with their TR Series and the Healey 100. Rootes would also join the fray the same year, initially with the first Sunbeam Alpine and then six years later with the second generation 'Series' Sunbeam Alpine.

The Sunbeam-Talbot 80 and 90 up-market saloons and Drophead Coupe, launched in 1948, were the first Rootes cars to move on from old pre-war designs and reflected the Rootes brothers' new interest in American-influenced design. Norman Garrad had worked for Sunbeam-Talbot and transferred to new owners Rootes. He had been a keen amateur rally competitor since the 1930s and started to privately rally the Talbot 90 with some success. This was despite it seeming an unlikely rally car, being rather heavy and with an

The Sunbeam-Talbot 90, the first post-war designed car that was manufactured by Rootes and the first Rootes car to have competition success. (Peter Laurence)

awkward column gear change. Garrad gradually gained factory support which evolved into the beginnings of the Rootes competition department. This department became an example for other manufacturers to follow in developing their own models for competition in motor sport. By the 1952 rally season the department had evolved so much as the result of the knowledge and experience gained in competition that it had attracted some gifted drivers, including rising star Stirling Moss. That year they gained some superb results in the Monte Carlo and Alpine rallies, and the Sunbeam-Talbot 90 also became a popular choice with privateers.

The Sunbeam-Talbot 90 led to the birth of the short-lived first-generation Sunbeam Alpine, initially developed by South Coast Rootes dealer and Rootes rally team member George Hartwell in 1952. He converted three Sunbeam-Talbot 90 convertible dropheads, modifying the bodywork to create hand-built cars he called the Sunbeam-Talbot Hartwell Coupe. Rootes liked it, recognising its rallying potential and also its ability to fill the gap for a sporty car in the Rootes range for the American market. There are several versions of events from here on, but it was decided to further develop and then produce it, the final result being a beautifully elegant two-seater. The 'Talbot' element of the name was dropped and 'Alpine' was chosen as a result of the close Rootes connection and success with the Alpine Rally in France. Henceforth the car became known as the 'Sunbeam Alpine', but it was also initially known as the 'Alpine Sport' and was referred to as such in early road test reports.

Launched in early 1953, this first-generation Alpine was first produced in left-hand drive for sale in the United States. A right-hand version followed later in the year. In March, to provide some publicity, an Alpine was prepared for Sheila van Damm and Stirling Moss to drive at Jabbeke in Belgium. It was common at the time for the new local road

The first-generation Sunbeam Alpine. (Steve Brown)

there to be closed and used for speed runs. With a special underbelly pan to reduce drag and an aero-screen fitted, Moss clocked up 119.126 mph and van Damm 120.135 mph. Sales, however, were slow. Both the road-going and modified rally versions of the Alpine, although more refined, were heavier, slower and more expensive than the rival Austin Healey, Triumphs and MGs. It did prove itself as a rally car, achieving great success in the 1953 and 1954 Alpine Rallies, again with Stirling Moss in the team. However, with disappointing sales, the car proved to be a commercial flop and production ended in 1955 with 1,282 Mark I and just 300 Mark III versions being produced (there was no Mark II).

The Sunbeam Rapier was introduced in late 1955. It was the first model of a new generation of Rootes cars from the 'Audax' range. These used modern monocoque

George Hartwell and co-driver Dr Bill Dean in the 1954 Alpine Rally, where they finished seventh in class. (Coventry Transport Museum)

The Sunbeam Rapier, a highly successful rally car, from which the Alpine borrowed its running gear. (Tony Fearn)

8

construction and a smaller newly designed 1,494cc overhead valve engine. Despite its new design, the Rapier was at first considered a rather comfortable but otherwise fairly average coupe and saloon car. To provide publicity and boost sales, the competition department were asked to see if they could develop the car for rallying without any big expectations. However, during the three years in progression to the Series III, the Rapier developed into a rugged, reliable performer and had major competition success.

With the introduction of the Audax range, the possibility of a new generation of Sunbeam Alpine was considered. With the potential to build on the reputation of Rootes' three previous sporting cars – the Sunbeam-Talbot 90, the first-generation Alpine and the Rapier – the Rootes brothers gave approval for a new design of sports model to be produced.

Serious work on the new model started in 1957, but an initial in-house design was turned down by the management. Kenneth Howes, a young British-born designer who had experience in America working on Studebakers and Fords, was then chosen to style the new model. With a minimal brief of a sports model but with more comforts than a traditional sports car, Howes had a free hand in the styling, with one exception. To make the project more practical and the final product more affordable, Rootes decided not to start development from scratch. The Alpine would use a modified version of the floorpan used for the Hillman Husky, a utility vehicle with a van-based profile. This meant the Howes styling had to conform to the Husky's rather short and not ideal 86-inch wheelbase. Howes produced a quarter-scale clay model which underwent successful wind tunnel tests at the Motor Industry Research Association. Work then progressed rapidly to a full-size wooden mock-up. This was completed in December and was uncharacteristically approved by the pernickety Rootes brothers without any alterations or modifications. It had clean, subtle, flowing lines – the boldest and most controversial feature being the American-influenced rear fins. The design had some further developments of the styling seen on the Mark I Ford Thunderbird and Studebaker Hawk, but had progressed so as to avoid their rather glittery flamboyance. Howes suggested Sunbeam Sabre as a name, but a reprise of the Sunbeam Alpine name was instead preferred by the Rootes brothers.

The Husky was originally based on the old Hillman Minx, but had been re-designed and introduced into the Audax range using the new Audax running gear. So the Alpine would

The Hillman Husky, which shared its floorpan design for use on the Sunbeam Alpine. (Kate Willock)

use the running gear of the latest Audax model, the Sunbeam Rapier Series III, which was under development at the same time. This included the transmission and the overhead valve 1,494cc engine with a new improved cast-aluminium cylinder head.

Alec Caine was project manager for the development programme, which saw a succession of five prototypes built in 1958 – two left-hand drive and three right-hand drive. Armstrong Siddeley were contracted to help with development. According to Alpine test driver Mike Adlington, the first prototype was built by him and other apprentices for use in a thorough testing programme focusing on the body shell. Dull grey in colour and with no attention-attracting badges, it was driven 60,000 miles in two months, in 8-hour shifts around the clock. Various selected drivers, including Mike, provided differing driving styles using five varying routes to test the car on different road surfaces and conditions. It is likely that three of the other prototypes were used just for experimentation with various interior and exterior features such as soft-top and hard-top designs, soft-top stowage, seating, styling and engine detail. Spotlights fitted on the fifth suggest it was used for some limited amount of road testing, which often took place after dark to avoid unwanted attention for new models.

Once testing of the first prototype was complete, the car was stripped down by Mike and his colleagues at the Armstrong experimental workshop and examined for wear and tear. Nothing of serious mechanical concern was found. At this point, though, it had not begun to become clear that the use of the Husky platform for an open-top car might lead to problems, since the roof section normally provided structural rigidity.

A further eight pre-production prototypes, registration numbers XRW 301 to 308, were built for the next stage of the testing programme, which was to be carried out by the road test engineers in the Rootes experimental department. Headed by Don Tarbun, with Bernard Unett as assistant manager, they were nicknamed 'the set 'em alight boys' due to Tarbun's phrase 'for **** sake, set 'em alight', often uttered when things went awry. According to Bernard Unett, XRW 302 was kept back for use by the styling department, but as soon as testing began on the rest of the cars the problem of body flexing on rough terrain, due to the lack of a roof to provide rigidity, was very apparent. The body flexing was tackled by experimenting with bracing crossmembers placed under the floorpan.

The principal road test experimental prototype Alpine parked outside the Armstrong-Siddeley experimental department. (Courtesy of Graham Robson)

Prototype WDU 807, probably at the Rootes Humber Road site (originally Hillman's factory), with a badly fitting experimental soft top featuring rear quarter-light windows that did not make it into production. (Chris McGovern Collection)

Prototype WDU 808 fitted with hard top was used for several photo shoots. No make or model badges are fitted. (Chris McGovern Collection)

Prototype WDU 427 looks pretty much like the production cars, and was possibly the final experimental prototype before the pre-production prototype test cars were built. (Chris McGovern Collection)

11

Prototype WRW 995 with experimental soft top, no peaks on the headlights and an open grill. Spotlights suggest it may have been used for some after-dark road tests so as to avoid unwanted attention. (Chris McGovern Collection)

Experiments with different thicknesses of crossmembers eventually yielded results that provided great rigidity while adding as little extra weight as possible. Peter Ware, who joined Rootes in 1958 as a chief engineer, tells a story of test driving a prototype Alpine and finding serious scuttle vibration on rough surfaces. He says this led to the now familiar struts being added, one on each side in the engine bay, which provided bracing between the front bulkhead and the wheel arches. This and other faults, he says, led production to be delayed for months until they were sorted out. However, Mike Adlington recalls the struts being added much earlier.

To continue extended testing of the pre-production prototypes they were sent to London, Scotland and the south of France. In London they were subjected to 8 hours of continuous driving in heavy traffic every day. This immediately showed a tendency for overheating, so the radiator matrix was changed from steel to copper, which seemed to solve the problem. Once all the cars had returned to the Coventry factory another problem became apparent. The Alpine was the first Rootes model to be fitted with front disc brakes. Every car had suffered heavy front brake pad wear and had mysteriously gone through two sets of brake pads while out on test. A great deal of time and effort was put in to finding the cause and rectifying this problem. On meeting Don Tarbun at Silverstone recently, he explained how he eventually arranged for an aperture to be cut in the wheel arch of an Alpine and covered with Perspex. This formed a window through which he could see exactly what was happening while the car was being driven. He found that any water present was being channelled directly into the brake assembly, with any grit it was carrying getting trapped and grinding down the pads. According to Tarbun, the problem was largely solved by altering the profile of the wheel arch. Research continued well after the Alpine was launched in order to fully rectify the fault with an effective splash guard.

Production

Because of a lack of capacity at the Rootes assembly plant in Coventry, and in exchange for help in developing the new Rootes engine for the Super Snipe, it was decided that as well as doing some of the development work, full initial production of the new Alpine would be sub-contracted to Bristol Siddeley Engines Ltd. Bristol Siddeley had been recently formed by the merger of Armstrong Siddeley Motors and Bristol Aero Engines. Uneconomic production of their only car, the Sapphire, was being wound down and about to end, so they had lots of spare capacity. A production line began to be set up in March 1959 in the Burlington works at the old Armstrong Parkside factory in Coventry, which Rootes already used for Minx body shell storage.

The Alpine was to be presented to the world's motoring press on the French Riviera on 2 July 1959, the day after the Alpine Rally ended and two days before the French Grand Prix, to ensure a good attendance. Workforce recruitment for the new production line began and by early May twelve pre-production models were nearing completion, eleven of which were destined for demonstration at the French launch. With the pre-production cars finished a few weeks before being revealed to the press, there was time for the rather tall project engineer, Alec Caine, to improve the interior by narrowing the seat backs to allow a bit more front leg room. Then eleven of the pre-production cars were prepared and, registered XVC 1 to XVC 11, were flown to France. After nearly being refused entry at customs, and then one car being damaged in a crash, the cars eventually reached Cannes just in time for the launch.

At the launch day in Cannes a recently honoured, now Lord, William Rootes announced the new model in front of a large gathering of motoring journalists and guests from all over the world. After an inspection of the cars, the journalists were able to try them out with an hour's drive up through the mountains, then back down to the coast near Saint Tropez. The day was rounded off with dinner for the remaining visitors. Jack Brabham was one of a handful of guests invited to keep an Alpine for an extended test period. He made good use of the car, appearing with it at the French and German Grand Prix, where he was competing in his Cooper-Climax. While in Germany, Brabham demonstrated the car on television at the Auvs track in Berlin and soon acquired one for his own personal use in Britain to replace the twin-carb Holden FC Special he had been using. He did a lot of promotional work for the Rootes Sunbeam marque and drove a 1904 Sunbeam in the 1959 London to Brighton veteran car run, helping to promote the new Alpine. Brabham continued promoting the Alpine by appearing regularly in press advertisements and writing magazine articles.

5 May 1959. Some of the pre-production cars being finished off in preparation for the launch day in Cannes on the new but otherwise empty production line. (Len Brooks)

Night-time testing of the pre-production Alpines. (Chris McGovern Collection)

Some of the pre-production cars, having arrived at Cannes on the launch day. (Chris McGovern Collection)

Lord Rootes (second left) at the Cannes launch, discussing the virtues of the Alpine. (Chris McGovern Collection)

Pre-production Alpine XVC 11 at the Cannes launch. (Chris McGovern Collection)

Jack Brabham with a 1904 Sunbeam. He was about to drive in the 1959 London to Brighton Car Run and is next to his own new Series I Sunbeam Alpine. (Coventry Transport Museum)

Press reviews were favourable. The Alpine looked good and was much more refined and better equipped than any of its obvious rivals. At around £971 it was also good value in comparison, although the hard top was £60 extra, as was overdrive. Motoring correspondents praised Rootes on their usual attention to detail. The interior was nicely finished with an aircraft-style instrument layout on the dash, wind-down windows and comfortable seats. The easily erected watertight soft top folded down completely out of sight behind a panel that formed the rear of the back seat, giving the Alpine the appearance of a roadster when the hood was down. Handling, performance and road holding were praised in road tests and the short Husky wheelbase did not seem to be a disadvantage, but the car just fell tantalisingly short of the magic 100 mph top speed. The aim of Rootes to combine luxury with good performance seemed to have been successful, but it was the very comfort of the car, its pretty appearance, and lack of blistering performance that would tend to mark it out in future as a sports tourer rather than a true sports car.

In October 1959 the Alpine was greeted with enthusiasm at the London International Motor Show at Earls Court, and Rootes provided the chance for motoring correspondents to put it through its paces on the race track at the Goodwood circuit. The good reviews and plentiful publicity produced a strong order book that led to more workers being taken on for a night shift to increase production, with much of the output going to America. A year later the order book was still bulging and management considered a £25,000 extension to the production line (half a million in today's money) to enable a double shift. This would have almost doubled production, but in the end it did not take place.

Motoring journalists who reported at the 1959 International London Motor Show at Earls Court were then given a chance to try the Alpine and other Rootes models on the track at Goodwood. (Coventry Transport Museum)

February 1960. A production line inspector checks the finish after painting. Body shells can rotate 360 degrees on specially designed trollies. (Len Brooks)

February 1960, the body finishing section of the production line in full swing. (Len Brooks)

October 1959, the roller test section on the production line. (Len Brooks)

September 1959, the final finishing section of the production line. (Len Brooks)

Alpine Series II

Rootes usually updated their models quite quickly, and the Series II Alpine was no exception. The Series II was introduced in October 1960 at the British International Motor Show at Earls Court, London. Improvements included increasing the cylinder bore of the engine to provide 1,592cc. This update was widely advertised, but even with a larger choke for the Zenith carburettors it really gave very little improvement in performance. There was improved legroom and a firmed-up rear suspension to improve the ride. The original stubby front window guide now went the full height of the raised window and there was a star-shaped petrol cap for easier removal.

Rootes did not want the extra noise that engine tuning would bring to production cars, so to make the Alpine more competitive they began to offer a wide selection of performance tuning parts. Kits were produced to allow for two stages of engine tuning. These were sold at spares stockists along with a tuning guide book. Jack Brabham had increased the engine performance using twin Webber 40 DCOE carburettors and hoped Rootes would take up the idea, but they rejected it after tests. This led Brabham to market a Weber conversion kit himself. He also pitched the idea of installing an American V8 engine in the Alpine

Jack Brabham with a Series II Alpine at the 46th International Paris Motor Show, held at the Grand Palais. (Coventry Transport Museum)

with the possibility of his own company modifying the standard production model. Rootes themselves experimented with fitting other engines, but none proved satisfactory.

As far as competition credentials were concerned, the Alpine had already enjoyed some rallying success. In the very tough 1959 RAC Rally two Alpines finished with reasonable placings, and in the 1960 Monte Carlo Rally an Alpine had finished first in class. In America an Alpine also won a production car series.

By the 1960s, strikes were becoming a central feature of British industrial relations – no more so than at Rootes. At the beginning of September 1961, unofficially and against union advice, a strike at the Acton-based Rootes steel pressing plant lost 27,000 man-hours in production. This led to 6,000 Coventry workers being laid off two and a half weeks later. Things went from bad to worse as the strike continued. With no body panels, production ground to a complete halt and 8,000 Coventry workers were made redundant. By the beginning of November the pressing of body panels had been contracted out by Rootes and production slowly resumed, with the workforce being rebuilt and strikers drifting back to work. But the two-month stoppage had put Rootes into the red and cost them millions of pounds at a time when they could least afford it, as much time and money was being invested in the continuing development of their new Hillman Imp and the new Imp factory in Scotland. Partly as an economy measure, Alpine production ended at Armstrong's Parkside factory in March 1962, moving to the Rootes Ryton-on-Dunsmore factory. All these factors led to an unusually long (for Rootes) two and half year gap between models: the Series II and Series III Alpine.

The genesis of the Tiger

When Ian Garrad, driving his highly tuned Sunbeam Alpine Series II, was reputedly casually out-accelerated by an old lady in a sedan, he began to think seriously about Brabham's idea of fitting a bigger engine that would dramatically improve performance. It was 1962 and Ian, son of Norman Garrad, was manager for Rootes on America's west coast. He found a likely candidate in the lightest V8 engine then able to fit under an Alpine bonnet, a Ford 4.2 litre unit. The following year, in March 1963, having secured funds from Rootes for the project, Garrad engaged engineers Carol Shelby and Ken Miles each to produce a prototype. The Ken Miles version was built very quickly and was rather crude, but demonstrated much potential. Shelby, having just had much success transplanting a Ford V8 into an AC Ace to produce the AC Cobra, took several months and used more adaptions to squeeze in the engine. The resulting car was pretty good, but still needed a lot of refinement which took some time. When Lord Rootes saw the resulting car in Britain in July he was impressed enough to approve it for production after securing a deal with Ford to supply the 3,600 engines a year that would be needed. 'Thunderbolt' had been the proposed name, but Lord Rootes decided on 'Tiger', after the name of Sir Henry Seagrave's land-speed record car. With lack of space for production at Rootes, Jensen were chosen to further develop the Tiger and later to produce it, with Shelby receiving a royalty for every car produced.

Alpine Series III

Although there had been significant production problems at the Rootes factories, research and development for the Alpine continued unhindered. It had been decided that there would be two versions of the Alpine Series III, with the introduction of a new, more luxurious GT version, fully carpeted and with a wooden dashboard and steering wheel. It had a detachable hard top but no folding soft top, giving additional room in the cockpit. The sports model had a slightly more powerful engine with larger inlet valves and, with the gear ratios altered, it was a bit nippier. But in making the GT as comfortable, quiet and refined as possible it ended up with a perceptively poorer performance than previous models. The hard top was redesigned, giving both models a much more modern look and, especially with the top fitted, a better interior – but with the disadvantage of the new steel top being heavier than the rounder aluminium top it replaced. The bodywork at the rear was altered to accommodate telescopic shock absorbers and there were a lot of other minor mechanical changes. Research into the front disc brake problem had finally resulted in an effective splash guard being developed.

Greatly improved seats, produced by aircraft seat makers Microcell, were introduced. These, combined with a new adjustable steering column system, provided a much more variable driving position. Italian coachbuilder Carrozzeria Touring had been assembling the Hillman Super Minx and Alpines for the Italian market for Rootes, apparently partly to avoid local import duties. They had also redesigned the Alpine's boot space and produced a handful of cars with much increased luggage space. This was achieved by positioning the

Sunbeam Alpine Series III GT at the Geneva Motor Show. (Coventry Transport Museum)

spare wheel in an upright position against the back of the rear seat and adding space-saving twin petrol tanks, one in each rear wing, with the petrol cap repositioned higher up. It was a big improvement which Rootes incorporated fully into production cars. Touring had also re-designed the exterior of the rear end and produced an Alpine with smaller cut-down fins, but Rootes held back this development from full production.

The Series III Sunbeam Alpine was launched in March 1963 at the Geneva Motor Show after a backlog of the orders for the Series II model was complete. Both versions of the Series III received favourable press reviews, the GT's lack of performance being partly overlooked because of its sumptuousness. The Alpine was now coming to be regarded as a well-finished car with some panache, but it really needed better performance to compete with the latest models of rival manufacturers. The Series III would be available for only ten months before being replaced by the Series IV.

Alpine Series IV

The Sunbeam Alpine Series IV was introduced in November 1963 by Carrozzeria at the Turin Motor Show. Rootes introduced the same model at the Brussels Motor Show in January 1964. Throughout 1963 big tail fins were quickly going out of fashion, so the Alpine appeared with the Carrozzeria Touring designed cut-down fins. It sported a newly shaped front grille, with one centrally placed horizontal bar and an oval centre badge replacing the louvred slat design. It also had smaller, more modern looking over-riders on the bumpers with rubber inserts. Combined side lights/indicators were no longer legal on new cars in Britain, so a new light cluster with separate indicator was fitted at the front. An oval, flush-fitting, lockable Monza-style petrol cap was also introduced. The lower powered GT engine refinements were scrapped, giving the GT the same power output as the Sports model, with a Solex carburettor replacing the previous twin Zeniths.

An automatic version of the Alpine was introduced using a Borg Warner three-speed automatic gearbox. Rootes figured it would appeal to the American market, but, being an auto, its performance was down compared with the manual model and it was the slowest Alpine yet. Large sales were projected for it, but it was a case of Rootes giving the Americans what they thought they needed instead of what they actually wanted, and only a few hundred were ever produced. Additional improvements followed in September, updating the gearbox and adding synchromesh on first gear so as to provide it on all forward gears. On the production line, body panels were modified so as to be able to skip the process of leading joins, speeding up production but also reducing costs.

The launch of the Tiger

Just a year after the Shelby prototype had been completed, the Tiger was on show to the public for the first time at the New York Motor Show in April 1964. Development had been extremely quick, with mass production at Jensen not getting underway until late June. Rootes were generally delighted with the reviews. *Autocar* reported a top speed of 117 mph and the 0–60 mph time was around 9 seconds, though it did vary between individual cars. The interior was pretty much the same as the well-appointed Alpine, apart from the stubby American-style gear lever. Without any exterior styling changes other than a thin chrome side strip, it also looked rather like the less powerful, less expensive Alpine on the outside, which was one problem that would detrimentally affect sales. It also faced stiff competition. In America, where most Tigers would be sold – initially for $3,499 – a Mustang was around $1,000 less expensive and a Corvette was only $300 more. Also, British sports car fans had the choice of Triumph's TR4, the Austin Healey 3000, the MGB GT and even the E-Type.

Having never recovered financially from the earlier strike and the disastrous reputation of the recently launched Hillman Imp, in which they had so heavily invested, the Rootes family entered talks with US car maker Chrysler in the spring of 1964 regarding some sort of amalgamation. In September Chrysler bought a non-controlling portion of shares in Rootes, but unfortunately, almost from the start, the partnership did not run smoothly. Chrysler now had connections with the recently launched Tiger, powered by an engine from rivals Ford. They did not seem to show a lot of interest in the Tiger's promotion or success, especially in America. Then, following a fall on holiday, Lord William Rootes became unwell at the Paris Motor Show in October and died just two months later from liver cancer, aged 70. Lord Rootes had been the driving force behind the business and his absence from the helm was soon to trigger big changes in the organisation. Sir Reginald Rootes succeeded his brother as chairman, but with the group being split into three operating divisions there were now many more executives making decisions that previously would have been taken by the family.

Alpine Series V

Series IV sales figures were down, so engineers had been working on a way to increase the Alpine's power and to successfully increase the engine capacity from 1,592cc to 1,725cc. Thinking it impractical to increase the bore any further they achieved this by lengthening the stroke and cleverly adding two extra bearings to the old three bearing design. There were other modifications, such as a new cam shaft and replacement of the unsatisfactory Solex carb with the better performing twin Stromberg carburettors, all producing around an extra 10 bhp. An alternator replaced the dynamo and an oil cooler was added. The soft-top stowage was redesigned with a more traditional clip-down vinyl cover over the lowered hood. With disappointing sales, production of the automatic version of the Alpine was ended before the Series V was launched in September 1965. The Hillman, Singer and Humber models that were to use the new 1,725cc engine were introduced shortly after. Alpine road tests published at the time reported no great improvement in performance, but, to most, this was the nicest, best built and fastest Alpine to be produced.

Tiger Mark II

December 1966 saw a new version of the Tiger, the Tiger Mark II, begin manufacture at the Jenson factory. The Mark II used a larger 4,727cc Ford engine, the original engine having ceased production. This gave it a hairy 7.5 second 0 60 mph time and a 125 mph top speed. To attempt to differentiate it from the Alpine, an egg crate grille was added as well as bright metal trim along the sills and wheel arches.

1966 saw the Rootes Group losses mounting to tens of millions of pounds, and it was now only a matter of time until Chrysler took overall control. This finally happened in January 1967. Not wanting to be just a figurehead, Sir Reginald Rootes resigned from his position as chairman. Within three years the use of the Rootes brand name, after what had been fifty years of motor sales and manufacturing, would be gone.

Selling the Tiger in America had been rather difficult, and with a Ford engine in what was now a Chrysler product and with no Chrysler engine being small enough to fit under the bonnet, the Tiger's future looked grim. Production ended within six months, as soon as the reserve of Ford engines were exhausted, with just over 600 Tiger II models having been produced, a little over 7,000 Tigers in all.

End of an era

With the Tiger gone, the Alpine's future was now under review, it being the last surviving model from the otherwise defunct Audax range that had been superseded by the new Arrow series. Chrysler finally ended production in January 1968 with an official total of just over 69,000 Alpines having been produced, although Rootes were never very good at keeping production records. There are particular discrepancies in figures when production was moved to the Ryton factory.

The Alpine name was brought back by Chrysler for a model in the Arrow range. In 1967 Chrysler introduced a very well equipped, fastback-style new Rapier model based on the Hillman Hunter. They went on to produce a very fast Holbay-engined H120 version. The Alpine was a nice, but less expensive, less powerful, and less well equipped version of the new Rapier.

Hybrids

Harrington Alpines

In March 1961 coach builders Thomas Harrington Ltd, a Rootes main dealer, launched their own version of the Alpine. It was a luxurious high-performance Grand Tourer using modified Alpine bodywork. Harrington Ltd was a firm of coach builders based in Hove, Sussex, which specialised in the use of glass fibre in coach building. With additional production capacity available, they decided to make a GT version of the Alpine using their techniques. Initially designed by Ron Humphries, three demonstration cars were made which Lord Rootes liked and approved for production. Harrington began with a stock Alpine and first altered and strengthened the floorpan then added a fastback-style glass fibre top, modifying the bodywork and the cockpit to produce a high-quality luxury interior. During development George Hartwell became involved in Harrington. This meant Hartwell's engine-tuning expertise would be employed in the production models. In all there were four versions.

The first was the Sunbeam Harrington Alpine and was based on the Series II Sunbeam Alpine. The glass fibre fastback-style roof extended down to the end of a shortened boot lid

A Sunbeam Harrington Alpine, based on the Series II Alpine. (Patricia Arculus)

and retained the fins. It was the best part of £200 more expensive than a standard Alpine supplied with a hard top. Around 110 cars were produced in varying trim as ordered by the individual customer. There was a choice of engine-tuning options by George Hartwell. Stage three involved twin Webber DCOE carburettors, giving a top speed of 110 mph. As an official conversion it was not seen in the showroom but was available from Rootes dealers as a special order. Harrington were then commissioned by Rootes to convert a car to enter at the 24 Hours of Le Mans race in 1961. Based on the Harrington Alpine, it had unique features such as faired-in headlights and a large undertray below the front valance to reduce drag. At Le Mans it did remarkably well, winning the prestigious Thermal Efficiency Cup.

The second model was named the Harrington Le Mans in recognition of the Alpine's victory at Le Mans and dropped the Alpine name tag. A small number of Harrington Alpines continued to be produced alongside the new model. The Harrington Le Mans was launched in October 1961 at the London Motor Show at Earls Court. Known as the Sunbeam Le Mans GT in America, it was also based on a Series II but with the rear fins completely removed, the rear wings gracefully sweeping down from the end of the door towards the rear bumper. The fastback roof had an opening rear hatch, and inside a folding rear occasional seat. With the seat folded down, a deceptively large luggage space was provided. The high price tag, £415 more expensive than the standard Alpine, which cost just over £1,000 with the optional hard top, resulted in less demand with just 250 cars being built, half going to America. It was an official Rootes product so was seen on showroom floors, with only a standard trim available in the USA.

The 'Series C' was launched a year later in October 1962, made alongside the Harrington Le Mans model. Still based on the Series II, it kept the fastback roof line and opening rear hatch but retained the fins at the rear. Engine tune and trim options were available and sold for only around £178 more than the Alpine supplied with hard top. Only around

A Harrington Le Mans publicity photograph showing off the elegant downward sweep of the tail end. (Chris McGovern Collection)

HRH The Duke of Gloucester with his Sunbeam Harrington Le Mans. The Tiger-style egg crate grille was an optional extra. (Coventry Transport Museum)

Just a handful of the Sunbeam Harrington Series D were produced on both the Alpine Series III and IV bodies. This is a Series III example. (Jim Bull/www.harringtonalpine.org)

The Harrington Le Mans had an occasional rear folding seat which, when down, turned the rear interior into a large luggage space. (Chris McGovern Collection)

twenty cars were built before Alpine Series II production ended in early 1963, thus becoming unavailable for conversion.

The modifications for the Series III Alpine, such as the change in slant of the windscreen to accommodate the new shape Alpine hard top, necessitated changes in the Harrington that led to the 'Series D'. The Series D was never officially launched. The first car was registered in July 1963. At most five cars were made on the Alpine Series III base. Five more cars were made on the Alpine Series IV base. A Harrington Tiger was produced as a one-off in early 1965.

Sunbeam Venezia

In October 1961 Rootes gave Italian coachbuilders Carrozzeria Touring a contract to assemble Alpines and Super Minxes for the Italian market. Touring produced around four Alpines and ten Super Minxes a day. Having a bulging order book with new contracts from Alfa Romeo, Lamborghini, and Maserati, they decided to build a new larger factory at Nova Milanese, Milan, which opened in 1962. They had redesigned the Alpine's pedals to provide more legroom and made other improvements which Rootes took up and included on the Series II, III and IV production cars. Touring had also produced a new design for a stretched four-seater version of the Alpine. In 1961, on seeing a model of the

A Sunbeam Venezia in a factory promotional photo. (Chris McGovern Collection)

This particular Sunbeam Venezia was the concours d'élégance winner at a show in Florence in May 1964. (Coventry Transport Museum Collection)

design, Sir William Rootes gave them the go ahead to produce a prototype. It was built on a Super Minx chassis using Touring's patented Superleggera (super lightweight) method, a tubular steel framework with aluminium body panels carefully kept separated to avoid electrolytic corrosion. Rootes approved the prototype, and after two months of testing and some modifications the Venezia, as it was named, went into production. 300 were to be manufactured on the Humber Sceptre chassis using a tuned version of the Rootes Sceptre 1,592cc engine with special cylinder head, camshaft and distributor, producing 88 bhp.

The Venezia was launched in early September 1963 in St Mark's Square, Venice, in front of many officials, the car having arrived rather precariously by gondola. Press reviews were reasonably good. The aluminium coachwork was exquisitely detailed and the interior comfortably trimmed, with a cabin resembling that of an aircraft. However, the Venezia, to be sold by Rootes in Italy, was rather expensive and exceeded the price of many much more powerful luxury cars. To help boost sluggish sales, the market was extended to most of Europe barring Britain, where import taxes would have made the price prohibitive. Things then conspired against both Touring and the Venezia. Financial problems at Rootes due to strikes, coupled with the Hillman Imp development and production costs, restricted Rootes' support for the Venezia. In addition, new Italian legislation was introduced that heavily taxed big-engined cars, which for Touring was most of their output. The final straw was a strike at the Touring factory. Around 200 Venezia models had been produced by the time production ended, Touring having to call in receivers in December 1966. Plans for a V8 and convertible versions, and even the possible use of the Venezia as a Rapier replacement, came to nothing.

International Rallying

Norman Garrad, always immaculately dressed and a keen amateur trial and rally competitor, originally worked for Rootes in sales promotions. With the introduction of the Sunbeam-Talbot 90 in 1948, he began to build an increasingly successful competition department after persuading the Rootes brothers that the publicity from successful competition would help increase sales. By picking and choosing events carefully, although rarely achieving an out-right win, there would usually be some sort of result that could provide good publicity. By 1950 the department had had some good placings in international rallies and had won the occasional prize. With the introduction of the more sophisticated Mark II Sunbeam-Talbot 90 their success grew, notably with the 1952

Sunbeam-Talbot 90 with John Cutts and John Pearman at the Marseilles control before the start of the 1951 Alpine Rally. (Coventry Transport Museum Collection)

Alpine Rally team. Garrad had the knack of attracting good drivers and was able to build an impressive team which included rising star Stirling Moss. On the third stage of the Alpine Rally, Moss's car lost part of the exhaust. After losing 26 minutes repairing the car, Moss incredibly made up the time and finished in tenth place, winning a Coupe des Alpes. In all, the team won the Manufacturer's team prize, three Coupes and the A. C. Challenge Cup. The Mark II became a popular choice for private entries, one of which, driven by Per Malling, gained Sunbeam's first outright victory in the 1955 Monte Carlo Rally.

The first-generation Sunbeam Alpine, developed from the Sunbeam-Talbot 90, only had a brief rally career but did prove itself to be a thoroughbred. The works rally cars had some thirty-six modifications made by the factory for competition, the 2,267cc engine producing 97.5 bhp. They took part in only two Rootes team rallies, the 1953 and 1954 Alpine Rallies. In 1953 four of six cars were awarded Coupes des Alpes for unpenalised runs, Stirling Moss and John Cutts finishing fourteenth overall and fourth in class, with Moss winning his second Coupe des Alpes. In 1954 Moss and Cutts came ninth overall and third in class. Moss won a third Coupe des Alpes and, along with it, the Alpine Coup d'Or – only the second driver ever to do so. Once all the cars were retired from rallying they were used by Rootes for promotional work. They were then sold off to whoever would buy them, several returning to classic rallying many years later.

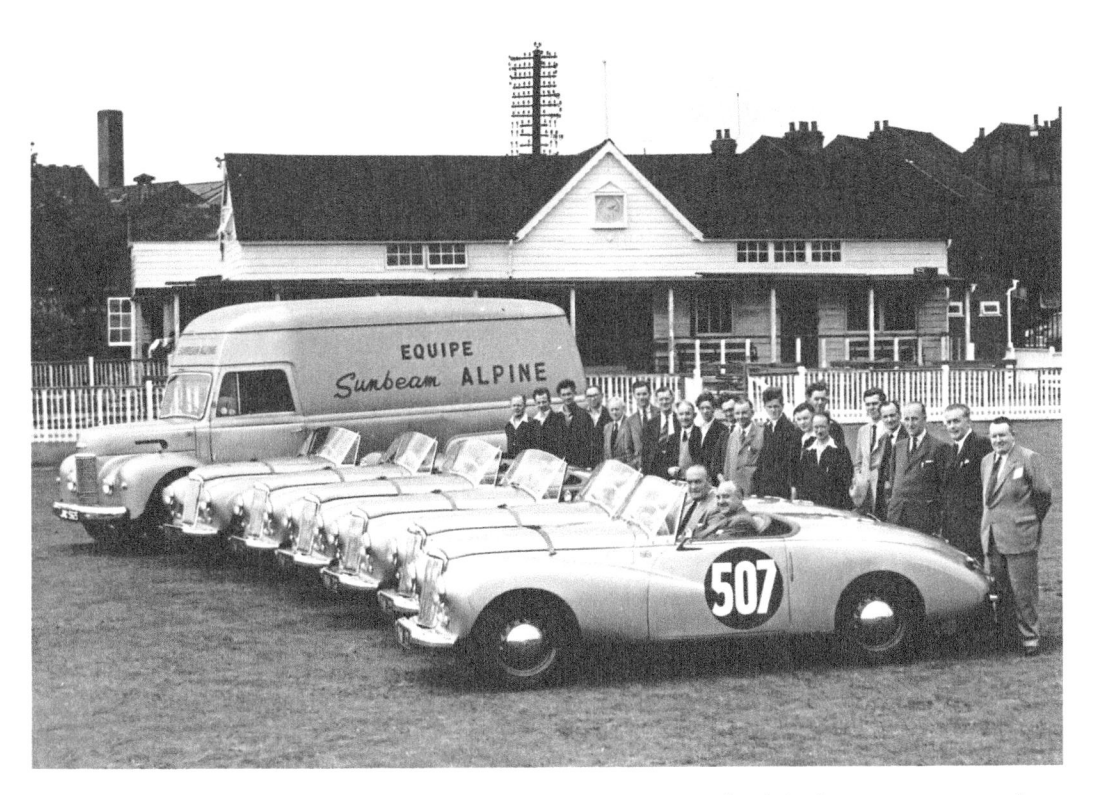

Norman Garrad at the wheel and Humber Director E. W. Handcock in the passenger seat of one of the six Sunbeam Alpines destined for the 1953 Alpine Rally. Behind them are engineers and mechanics from the Ryton-on-Dunsmore and Stoke factories who helped build and tune the cars. (Coventry Transport Museum)

From left to right: John Cutts, Peter Miller, George Murray-Frane and John Pearman about to board a Silver City Airways transporter with Sunbeam Alpines to compete in the 1953 Alpine Rally. (Coventry Transport Museum)

Stirling Moss and John Cutts on arrival at Cannes in their Alpine after completing the Alpine Rally without loss of marks, winning the Coupe Des Alpes. (Coventry Transport Museum)

Having introduced the Rapier in October 1955, Rootes wanted a sporting image for the car to help boost sales. Although seemingly just an average saloon car, the competition department immediately started work to try and make it competitive without any big expectations. Six months later it was ready for its first event, the Mille Miglia in Italy. Cruising at a speed of around 100 mph, Peter Harper and Sheila van Damm finished in seventy-second place and fourth in class, in a race in which only half of the 365 starters actually finished. Another Rapier finished fifth in class, sixteen places behind them. The following year Harper managed to finish second in the Special 1,600cc Touring Class with Jackie Reese. There was a class win for Jimmy Ray in the Tulip Rally in 1957, then Peter Harper, who had become the rally team captain, won the RAC Rally outright in 1958. The Rapier also won the first five places in class in the Alpine Rally the same year. By this time, Garrad had become the top rally team manager of his day and had become a hugely respected figure. In a publicity coup, he had somehow managed to sign the new Formula One World Champion Mike Hawthorn to drive a Hillman Husky in the 1959 East African Safari. Tragically, Hawthorn was then killed in a motor accident on the Guildford bypass. Paddy Hopkirk got a big break by stepping in, joining the team to rally the Husky and then a Rapier, coming third on the Alpine Rally. The Rapier carried on and enjoyed an illustrious career in competition with dozens of other victories, peaking in 1961.

Five Rapiers entered the 1959 RAC Rally with Hopkirk and Harper among the Rootes drivers. With the prospect of giving the Alpine a similar sporting image, and to exploit the Rapier connection, a works Alpine was also prepared (although kept in pretty standard form) to assess its potential. The rally took place only four months after the car's introduction. The Alpine was driven by Jimmy Ray with Phil Crabtree as co-driver. Another Alpine was privately entered by Rootes dealer Alan Fraser with Shenley-Price as

The Sunbeam Rapier team – 1958 Alpine Rally. From left to right: Peter Harper and Peter Jopp, Tommy Sopwith and Bill Deane, David Humphrey and Raymond Baxter, Mary Handley Page and Ivor Buep, Lola Grounds and Jimmy Ray, George Hartwell and Tiny Lewis. (Coventry Transport Museum)

co-driver. Starting at Blackpool, *Motor Sport* magazine chronicled Fraser's bad start with his poor manoeuvring in the test on the Blackpool seafront. Heading north through the Lake District to Scotland, heavy snow at the pass to Braemar trapped some of the leading drivers, including Ray, resulting in a 300 point penalty for missing the Braemar control point. Fraser, along with other later arrivals, managed to circumnavigate the pass to dodge the logjam, going off the official route without penalties. Stopping for tests at circuits such as Aintree, Oulton Park and Brands Hatch, the 2,000 mile course, covered in three and a half days, ended at Crystal Palace in London. The Fraser Alpine finished third in class and Ray's Alpine, further down the field, fifth in class among fifty-three of the original 131 starters. With their otherwise impressive top performance, Ray and Crabtree would have finished much higher up the rankings had they not got stuck in the snow at Braemar.

With the RAC Rally having demonstrated the Alpine's abilities, there was enough encouragement to muster eight private Alpine entries for the 1960 Monte Carlo Rally. They were all prepared with Hartwell stage II tuned engines. The rally covered 2,350 miles in seven days, with stages starting in various places such as Oslo, Lisbon, Glasgow, Frankfurt and Paris. Car number 113, driven by Olle Persson with Kalle Ridderbourg as navigator and co-driver, crashed off the road 125 miles from Grenoble and was forced to retire. Car 48 with Helge Josefsson and Karl-Erik Anderson suffered fuel contamination and only got as far as Grenoble. However, the Rune Backlund and Nils Falk team in a Swedish-entered Alpine qualified for the last rally stage to Monte Carlo and managed to finish first in the Grand Touring Car class (1,300–2,000cc) and thirty-first overall, also winning five other cups in the process. The win was despite being rather disadvantaged by the handicapping system, which would continue to hamper results. Peter Harper and Raymond Baxter also managed a win in the Production Touring Car class in a works Rapier.

Rune Backlund and Nils Falk in the Swedish-entered Alpine on its way to a class win (1,300–2,000cc) in the 1960 Monte Carlo Rally. (Chris McGovern Collection)

In spite of the showing of initial promise, the competition department with its limited budget and resources decided to concentrate on rallying the Rapier, which had a better chance of good results without the handicapping disadvantages of the Alpine. With larger production numbers the Rapier was also more in need of the sporting reputation to help sales, whereas the Alpine was selling well on its good looks and urbane qualities alone. So through the early 1960s the Alpine was destined only for the occasional appearance as a works entry in international rally events. However, thanks to private entrants taking up the challenge, the Alpine still made many appearances in international rallying over the next four years. Records are poor and sometimes inaccurate, but the following is an account of some of the best recorded events.

Backlund and Falk entered the 1961 Monte Carlo Rally and again finished first in class, also winning the Beach Cup, but with the ridiculous handicap system were placed eighty-fourth overall. An Alpine driven by Leir and Walters finished ninety-sixth overall and second in class. The Alpine was represented in the Alpine Rally in both 1960 and 1961 by Mary Handley Page. The first attempt in an Alpine, registered 6969 EL, with Pat Oxanne as co-driver netted third in class and twenty-second overall. In 1961 Handley Page (again with Oxanne) achieved another third in class and second place in the Coupes des Dames, in the same car, which had undergone Harrington conversion.

John Melvin, a Rootes main dealer in Scotland, was a private entrant in the 1961 International Scottish Rally with his wife Anne as co-driver. He prepared his Alpine with an engine that had been sent to Rootes for factory special tuning. A combination of hill climbs, special sections, driving tests, and some long fast stages with difficult mountainous sections severely tested both car and driver. Melvin's care and skill through the special stages and driving tests put him among the front runners and the speed of the Alpine gave him the fastest time through

Mary Handley Page and Pat Oxanne with their converted Harrington Alpine, 6969 EL, and the Rapiers that made up the rest of the 1961 Alpine Rally Team. (Coventry Transport Museum)

Mary Handley Page and Pat Oxanne in the Gavia Pass, in the Swiss Alps, in the 1960 Alpine Rally. (Chris McGovern Collection)

two of the long mountain sections. At the end of the fourth day Melvin had taken the lead. He managed to hang on to it during the fifth and final day's driving test and road stage, securing a class win and also winning the rally outright. On returning home Melvin found a message from Rootes apologising for the mistake of returning the incorrect, un-tuned engine to him. Much to his surprise, Melvin had won the Scottish Rally in a completely standard Alpine!

Spurred on by his success, Melvin decided to enter the 1962 RAC Rally. This time he would be using a red George Hartwell-tuned Harrington Le Mans, registered 2 EGG. W. Gordon Bennett was to be his co-driver and the car was delivered early enough for them to try it out on the International Scottish Rally in June. Things did not run smoothly and they were forced into retirement when the Harrington's electrics got soaked while crossing a deep ford. All set for the RAC Rally and hoping for better luck, W. Gordon Bennett then had to pull out of the event due to the sudden death of a work colleague. Luckily, Graham Gauld, editor of *Motor World* magazine and an experienced co-driver, was able to step in at short notice to take Bennett's place. By coincidence, Alan Fraser had also entered his red Harrington Le Mans, registered MEL 63, driven by Peter Pillsworth and Gregor Grant, the editor of *Autosport* magazine. Works ex-Le Mans Alpine 9202 RW was also entered, driven by the new Rootes ladies' crew of Rosemary Smith and Rosemary Seers, their added glamour providing a sure way for Rootes to get extra publicity and press coverage. No less than sixteen Rapiers were also entered, with drivers including Alan Fraser, Peter Procter, Andrew Cowan and Peter Harper, who had Rootes competitions chief Norman Garrad as co-driver.

The forestry roads on the first night's stage were very rough. Procter had the exhaust ripped off his Rapier and Peter Harper crashed out after his headlights failed and he hit a

John Melvin and Graham Gould in Harrington Le Mans 2 EGG in the 1962 RAC Rally. (Chris McGovern Collection)

The Alan Fraser-owned Harrington Le Mans MEL 63 in action in the 1963 RAC Rally. (Coventry Transport Museum)

tree in the dark. Peter Pillsworth's Harrington hit a rock, but got going again with a smashed headlight and damaged wing. Melvin's Harrington suffered a similar fate and limped to the end of the stage with smashed rear shocks. Once repaired, yet another rock ripped his petrol tank, which they patched with some chewing gum. Limping on for two more stages, the tank was then repaired. But it was not to last for long. With the car bottoming out again, the tank was damaged for a second time and the metal fuel line squashed flat, putting the car out of the rally. Rosemary Smith did finish, but well down the field. The best placed Rootes entry was Tiny Lewis in a Rapier, with Erik Carlsson's Saab eventually winning overall for the third year running. 1965 saw Melvin enter a Sunbeam Tiger in the Scottish Rally with better luck, coming away with a class win for Grand Touring cars.

For the 1962 Monte Carlo Rally Gregor Grant and Cliff Davis entered a previously successful ex-Le Mans racer, Alpine registration number 3001 RW. Drivers Rosedale and

Sunbeam Alpine 3001 RW swaps roles from racer in the 1961 Le Mans to rally car for the 1962 Monte Carlo Rally. (Chris McGovern Collection)

Rossdale and Freeman with their Alpine in the 1962 Monte Carlo Rally. (Chris McGovern Collection)

40

Freeman entered 5269 MP, and John Melvin entered an Alpine, 2 BUS, with co-driver W. Gordon Benett. Paddy Hopkirk finished third overall in a Rapier with two other Rapiers in the top ten. Melvin's Alpine finished third in class and Grant's car fifth in class, with Rosedale's car finishing further down the field.

1963 saw the ladies' team of Smith and Sears driving a works entered Rapier in the Monte Carlo Rally. Gregor Grant with journalist Tommy Wisdom borrowed the Alpine used the previous year by the ladies' team on the RAC Rally but did not do well, running out of

John Melvin and Gordon Benett on their way to a third in class in the 1962 Monte Carlo Rally. (Chris McGovern)

Monte Carlo Rally 1962. Gregor Grant and Cliff Davis finish fifth in class in Alpine 3001 RW. (Coventry Transport Museum)

41

Rossdale and Freeman, between stages in the Monte Carlo Rally 1962. (Chris McGovern Collection)

The 1963 Monte Carlo Rally. Using one of the Kamm-tailed Le Mans cars between races, Gregor Grant and Tommy Wisdom struggled in bad weather and failed to finish. Research by Rod Wallis shows that 9202 RW changed registration numbers, so this car actually appeared as 9201 RW at Le Mans in 1962. (Chris McGovern Collection)

time. Conditions were terrible, with the snow forming a complete 'white out'. Rosemary Smith rolled the Rapier down a bank and Seers was knocked unconscious. They were rescued by Mercedes competitor H. Felder who stopped to give assistance. He took them both to hospital, but lost so much time he put himself out of the rally. The Rapier of John La Trobe got snowed in, but Peter Harper and Ian Hall managed to finish in seventeenth place overall in their works-entered Rapier.

Irish Rootes dealer Charles Eyre-Maunsell entered and drove a pretty much standard Sunbeam Alpine in the 1960 International Circuit of Ireland, a 1,500 mile event traditionally held over Easter. The car performed well on the fast stages but did lack manoeuvrability on some of the tighter driving tests. The second stage of the rally was a difficult timed section with eleven control points and the Alpine was one of the few cars to get through with no penalties. It had the power to secure third place overall behind two rather heavier Austin Healy 3000s in a closing uphill stage. Unfortunately Eyre-Maunsell made errors on the very last stage, collecting 225 penalty points, and finally finished third in his class. He entered the event for another four years but never managed to improve on his 1960 placing.

Tiny Lewis drove an Alpine on the 1963 RAC Rally but did not get very far, retiring on the second stage with a holed petrol tank. A final works team attempt was more successful. The ladies' team consisting of Rosemary Smith and recently recruited co-driver Margaret MacKenzie entered the 1963 Tour de France, in which they won the Coupe des Dames. It was a combination of public road sections, hill climbs and circuit racing all over France

Charles Eyre-Maunsell with his 1960 Circuit of Ireland Alpine. (Chris McGovern Collection)

Rosemary Smith (driving) and Margaret MacKenzie at the start of the Geneva Rally 1964, the first international rally in Europe that Sunbeam Tigers had entered. The Tigers took the first three places in the over-2,500cc class. (Coventry Transport Museum)

over eight days. Again using a recent ex-Le Mans racer, they were one of only thirty-one finishers out of a field of 122 starters. They beat off stiff competition, coming sixth overall in the Grand Touring category ahead of eight Porsches, three Abarth Simcas and a whole team of Renault Alpines in the same class.

With the V8 Tiger on the horizon to develop for rallying, that was the end of any works interest or involvement in international events for the Alpine. In 1964 the Tiger took the first three places in the Grand Touring car class in the Geneva Rally (missing out on the manufacturers' prize when Rosemary Smith got lost just before reaching the finishing line) and a fourth place overall in the 1965 Monte Carlo Rally. As a result of technical problems, changing regulations and the move towards non-tarmac surfaces, which did not suit any of the low-slung sports cars, the Tiger never had any further significant works success as a rally car. With most of its technical problems (especially overheating) eventually sorted out, it was disqualified from its one big victory on the Alpine Rally in 1965 for having non-standard, smaller valves in the cylinder head – an inadvertent mistake made when the competition department prepared the car. The Tiger was withdrawn from works entries in 1966 after competing in the Acropolis Rally, coming first in the GT Class, seventh overall.

International Racing

In 1959 Rootes decided that the competition department should enter some cars in track events to add some extra sporting glamour to tempt buyers. What really sold the sports car dream was being able to imitate your racetrack hero. 'Win on Sunday, Sell on Monday', was the mantra. Although mainly competing in rallying, competition manager Norman Garrad did have experience in successfully racing big Talbots at Brooklands. A works-prepared Sunbeam Rapier was raced by the Rootes competition department's Mike Parkes in all eight rounds of the following year's British Saloon Car Championship. The car performed well, but Parkes was out of the top results. In November, Peter Harper and Paddy Hopkirk both drove works-entered Rapiers in a race at the 1960 American sports car Grand Prix meeting at the Riverside International Raceway in California. Harper shot into third place at the start of the race, closely followed by Hopkirk. Harper held his position, coming an

Paddy Hopkirk in one of two Sunbeam Rapiers that competed at Riverside in 1960. (Henry Ford Collection)

impressive first in class, and third overall behind two Jaguars, with Hopkirk retiring after an axle broke. The Rodriguez brothers later raced both Rapiers in Mexico and one of the cars took part in the Marlboro 12-hour race. Harper took over from Parkes for the 1961 and 1962 British Saloon Car Championship seasons and performed well, finishing in seventh and second place overall respectively, with a respectable class win in 1962.

Norman Garrad lined up two track events for the Alpine, the 1961 Sebring 12-hour endurance race in Florida and the 1961 Le Mans 24 hours endurance race. Lord Rootes was dubious about entering endurance racing, particularly Le Mans, and the Rootes engineering director was dead against it, but Garrad pointed out that the Le Mans 24 hours was well recognised in America and would help sales. Garrad volunteered to organise a test run, hiring the Silverstone circuit in February to determine the reliability of the Alpine in endurance events. Test drivers Harper and Procter also remember testing at the Motor Industry Research Association's test track at Lindley. The tests proved successful, showing the Alpine well able to withstand the punishment of up to 24 hours of racing, so Lord Rootes gave the go-ahead for some Alpines to compete.

Three factory-prepared Series II Alpines were entered to race at Sebring on 25 March. There would be a good chance of beating main rivals MG and getting a class win. Norman Garrad and a pit crew, along with three Wedgewood Blue Alpines, arrived in good time for some practice at the Sebring track, a rather rough outer ring of an old American air force

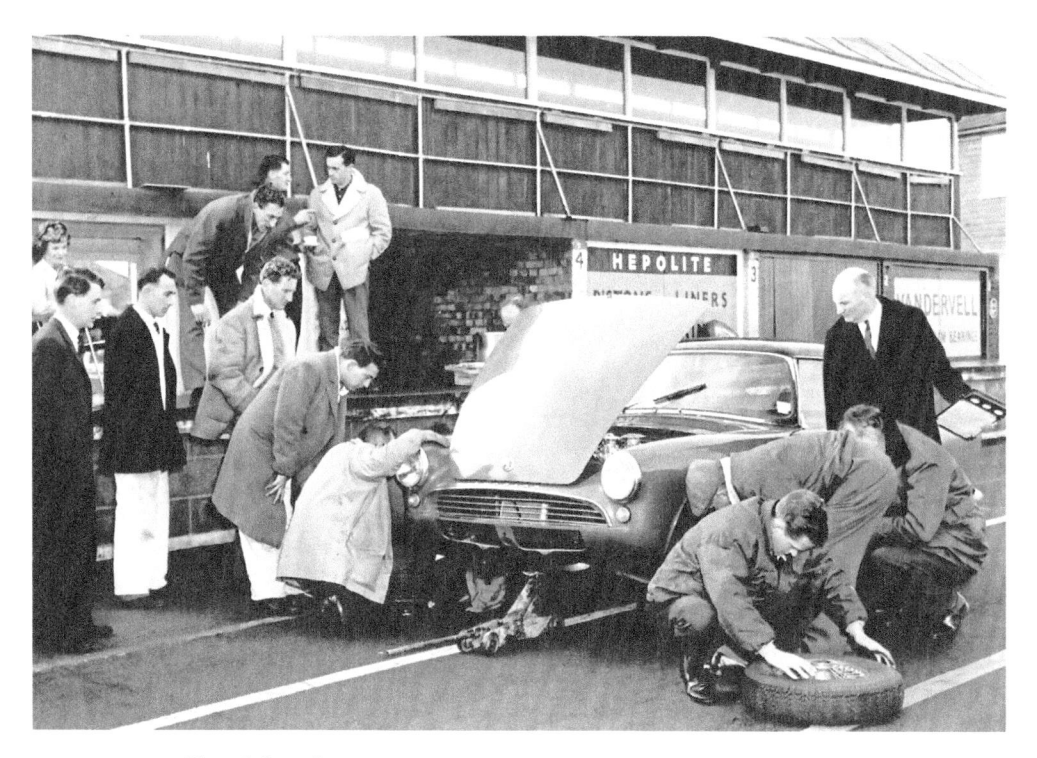

Norman Garrad hired the Silverstone circuit in February 1961 for a dawn to dusk session, testing the Alpine to see if it would stand up to endurance racing. Raymond Baxter is on the wall leaning forward, Peter Harper in front, Peter Procter behind. Norman Garrad is on the right in the overcoat. (Chris McGovern Collection)

base in Florida. Filippo Theodoli, an executive for Gardner Advertising, also entered an Alpine. Starting at 10 a.m., in front of a large crowd, the works team began surprisingly well. With a quarter of the race completed, two of the Alpines had unexpectedly built

Alpines in position for the start of the 1961 Sebring 12-hour race. (Davey Jordan Collection)

The Harper/Procter Alpine makes a good start. (The Revs Institute of Automotive Research)

up a good class lead in front of the well proven 1,600cc MGAs. However, then came the first of several disastrous pit stops. It took around 6 minutes for the Rootes mechanics to change tyres and refuel. The trailing MGA's pit stop took only 80 seconds, badly denting Rootes' initial lead. The Alpine driven by Americans Ed Wilson and Vince Tamburo then had to retire with engine trouble. The Peter Harper/Peter Procter Alpine then had an unscheduled pit stop to sort out braking problems, letting through the two closely following MGAs into first and second place. The MGAs held on to their lead, eventually winning their class, the Alpines unable to catch up after having even more unscheduled stops. The Harper/Procter car still managed to finish third in class, seventeenth overall. The third Alpine, piloted by Paddy Hopkirk and Peter Jopp, limped in at thirty-fourth

Left: Overly long pit stops eroded the Alpine's initial class-leading position, letting MG through to beat them. (Davey Jordan Collection)

Below: The Wilson/Tambouro Alpine being hotly pursued by Bud Gates in his Chevrolet Corvette. Some evidence now suggests this Alpine was prepared in the US. (Revs Institute of Automotive Research)

place after a long pit stop for head gasket repairs. The Filippo Theodoli Alpine came in thirty-first, sixth in class. Unfortunately, the inexperience of the Rootes team had resulted in them embarrassingly throwing away a likely victory. It would be vital to perfect their pit routine before the next big race.

The idea of Rootes entering the 24 Hours of Le Mans, the 'Grand Prix of endurance and efficiency', was supposedly first suggested by a Rootes concessionaire based in France. Norman Garrad first had to get some financial backing through his connections with the likes of Dunlop, Champion and Shell to help fund the project and build three cars. Manufacturing of the new Harrington version of the Alpine was just getting under way, so it was decided that one of the race cars should be a Harrington, while the other two cars would be of standard body shape. With George Hartwell in charge of the project, the Harrington featured the fastback-style rear but with a unique specially modified rounded aluminium nose with recessed faired-in headlights to reduce drag. The other two cars featured some weight-saving aluminium body panels. Garrad recalls taking a team of engineers and two cars to Le Mans for testing in April where they qualified for the race, which was scheduled for June. The test results were a bit disappointing, and with the speeds the Alpines managed to attain it was unlikely that they would be able to gain first place in their class. Running as production entries, they had to stick with the 1.6 litre production engine that had already been tuned to its limit. However, a reasonable finishing position would still provide plenty of good publicity. In a letter in which he wrote about the race, Garrad explained that he had a hunch and, although keeping it quiet, was mindful of another possibility of collecting some silverware.

Having now honed the pit stops to perfection, the team arrived at Le Mans allowing a week for practice sessions and rehearsal. Unfortunately both cars were slower in practice than on their test run in April. They literally scraped through 3 hours of scrutineering, the mechanics having to over-inflate the tyres to get the drag-reducing undershields over the ground clearance test. The Alpines also failed the suitcase test for available boot

Final practice, the day before the 1961 Le Mans 24-hour race. From left to right: Lewis Garrad, Peter Harpper, Tiny Lewis (behind pit wall), David Bodkin, Paddy Hopkirk and Norman Garrad in the Sunbeam pits. Hopkirk explains the Harrington Alpine's handling during practice to Bodkin, Rootes chief experimental engineer. (Coventry Transport Museum)

capacity, but the team argued it out with the scrutineers, just as they had seen the Porsche team do when they had the same problem. With a crowd of 250,000 on race day, the cars were lined up for the nerve-racking, accident-prone start at 4 p.m., where drivers had to sprint across the track to their cars at the drop of the starting flag. Both cars got away safely with the standard-shaped Alpine driven by Paddy Hopkirk and Peter Jopp proving to be much quicker than the Peter Procter/Peter Harper-driven Harrington Alpine. This brought into question whether all the bodywork modifications had made any difference at all, although the standard Alpine had a slightly higher revving engine. Both cars were running perfectly, just stopping for fuel. Then after 12 hours the Hopkirk/Jopp car suffered engine problems which led to its disqualification for the addition of oil by the pit crew before the allowable minimum distance had been reached. The Harrington car kept going, moving up twenty-two places from its halfway position. The pit crew did not realise, until

Both Alpines get away safely at the accident-prone sprint start of the 1961 Le Mans 24-hour race. (Coventry Transport Museum)

Peter Harper and Peter Procter very nearly beat the record for least time spent in the pits. (Chris McGovern Collection)

it was pointed out to them by the Aston Martin team, that the Harrington was leading in the Index of Thermal Efficiency – awarded to the most fuel efficient car. Garrad's hunch was proving to be right and he carefully paced the car to conserve fuel for the remainder of the race. To the competition team's surprise, the Harrington carried on to win the prestigious Index of Thermal Efficiency Cup. This was second in importance to the overall

Right: The Harrington Alpine being followed by the Graham Hill/Stirling Moss Ferrari 250 GT Berlinetta SWB of the North American/RRC racing team, which failed to finish, suffering a water leak. (Chris McGovern Collection)

Below: The Harper/Procter Harrington Alpine finishes to win the Index of Thermal Efficiency. (Chris McGovern Collection)

winner's prize and they had beaten Porsche, the expectant victors. Finishing sixteenth overall, second in class, the Alpine proved to be the fastest true production car at Le Mans, averaging 18 mpg, lapping at an average speed of around 91 mph, and attaining over 115 mph along the Mulsanne straight.

Following the great publicity from the Le Mans cup win and good results from national championships in America, Norman Garrad arranged for a hurriedly prepared Rootes car to race with other Alpines in 1961 3-hour endurance race at the Sports Car Grand Prix meeting at the Riverside Raceway in California. The race was technically an amateur event because it was sponsored by the California Sports Car Club, but I have included it here because of its international flavour and the international status of the race the following day, where Jack Brabham and Stirling Moss were taking part using some bigger machinery in the Grand Prix for sports cars. Brabham drove an Alpine that was lent by California Rootes dealer Bud Rose. The car had been raced regularly for Rose by Steve Froines in Sports Car Club of America events with great success. Moss had been hired by Garrad

1961 Riverside 3-hour sports car race Grand Prix. Jack Brabham, Norman Garrad and Stirling Moss prepare for the race. In America the rules allowed aero screens to be fitted for club racing. (Coventry Transport Museum)

The start of the 1961 3-hour race at Riverside. (Henry Ford Collection)

to drive the Rootes-prepared car. Unfortunately it overheated in the very short practice session, so it was arranged that Moss would share Brabham's car, driving the final hour. It would be Brabham's first of a number of production sports car races with the Alpine, a great publicity coup for Rootes. Ralph Bowyer raced in his own Alpine, an ex-factory car from the Sebring race. Ken Miles and Rootes dealer Lew Spencer also drove their own cars. Despite being hurriedly set up with too much understeer for Brabham's liking, he surged ahead at the start of the race and gained and held a class-leading position in fourth place overall, attaining 108 mph on the main straight. After starting well, Lew Spencer was bumped early on, necessitating a pit stop for a new rear tyre. Back on the track he then collided with an Alfa, losing 25 minutes on another pit stop for radiator repairs. Ralph Bowyer was forced to retired after misjudging a bend early on and crashing off the track into some spectators, who luckily were not badly hurt. Miles retired at around the halfway

Lew Spencer returns to the race after repairs to the radiator caused by a car in front of him skidding, causing a collision. (Coventry Transport Museum)

Stirling Moss roaring out of the pits after swapping the wheel with Jack Brabham, going on to third place overall and a class win. (Coventry Transport Museum)

53

point with braking problems. Although being clocked just a second short of the class lap record after his pit stops, Spencer came in last. Moss, having taken over from Brabham, masterfully overtook the third-placed car before the end of the race, taking a first in class and finishing third overall. Rootes were delighted with this valuable demonstration of reliability ahead of a Lola, a 2-litre Maserati, a Lotus Mark XII and many other more powerful cars, with two of the biggest names in the sport. It greatly improved the Alpine's racing credentials and got lots of publicity that provided a big boost in American sales. The Brabham/Moss car (actually not the real car but a replica) was subsequently displayed with great ceremony at the Los Angeles International Auto Show. As with the Sebring Alpines, Rootes sold off the factory car. They all subsequently took part in various Sports Car Club of America events. The car Stirling Moss was originally supposed to drive was sold to Ray

A replica of the Brabham/Moss class-winning Alpine on display at the 1961 Los Angeles International Auto Show. Model Carol Lytton is holding a jewelled spanner aloft. (Chris McGovern Collection)

The 1962 3-hour Riverside Sports Car Grand Prix race team in the paddock. Ted Bloch's Alpine is in the foreground originally the Harper/Procter 1962 Sebring car. (Davey Jordan Collection)

Ray Pickering in the 1962 Riverside 3-hour race. He had an innovative helmet with a radio mic that allowed him to talk to the pits. This car is the former Rootes-prepared Alpine Stirling Moss intended to drive the previous year, which Pickering had bought and then raced for several years. (Coventry Transport Museum)

Jack Brabham in the 1962 Riverside 3-hour race, where he finished in fourteenth place. (Coventry Transport Museum)

Bruce McLaren drove Lew Spencer's Alpine *Baby Doll II* in the 1962 Riverside 3-hour race, where he finished in fifteenth place. (Coventry Transport Museum)

55

Pickering, who raced it successfully for several years, racking up over twenty-five first and second places.

The 1962 Riverside 3 Hours saw six private Alpine entries. Ken Miles had the best result coming sixth, second in class behind a Porsche 356, with Ray Pickering's Alpine in seventh place directly behind Miles. Jack Brabham and Bruce McLaren finished fourteenth and fifteenth with Ted Block and Jerry Titus failing to finish in Peter Harper's 1962 Sebring car.

A team of three Seacrest green works Alpines were to return to Sebring with Norman Garrad in March 1962 for the 12-hour race. They were factory prepared with aluminium doors, bonnet and boot-lid panels and modified tail lights. For quicker refuelling they were fitted with oversize fuel filler lines protruding through the hard top, with a large filler cap sticking out the rear window. Filippo Theodoli was also competing for a second year running, this time as part of the team driving a Sunbeam Harrington. A class win would be more unlikely than the previous year because of stiffer competition from Porsche and TVR. However, entering the race with a reasonable end result would provide publicity, especially if they could beat rivals MG. At the start of the race Peter Harper (again teamed with Peter Procter) took a hard knock when a Corvette Stingray driven by Don Yenko crashed into him on the first corner, pushing him off the track. With just bodywork damage, Harper was still able to surge ahead and pass Ken Miles to take the lead among the Alpines. They battled with the MGs and TVRs for the whole of the race but were unable to catch two Porsches driven by Gurney and Barth, well ahead in the class lead. Harper overtook

The 1962 Sebring team. From left to right: Norman Garrad, Peter Procter, Peter Harper, Ken Miles, Lew Spencer, Tom Payne, John Panks, Jo Sheppard, Freddie Barrett, Filippo Theodoli. (Davey Jordan Collection)

Above: Alpines lined up for the start of the Sebring 12-hour race 1962. (Davey Jordan Collection)

Right: Peter Harper's Alpine at the 1962 Sebring 12-hour race after being side-swiped on the first corner. (Chris McGovern Collection)

Below: The Ken Miles/Lew Spenser Alpine, pictured before colliding with an O.S.C.A. and being forced to retire. (Chris McGovern Collection)

The Payne/Sheppard/Spencer Alpine with the Ferarri 250 Testa Rossa of George Constantine. (Davey Jordan Collection)

Parkinson's MG-A and began tailing Cuomo's TVR. In a quick pit stop Procter swapped with Harper, and Procter then pressured the Coumo TVR so much it suffered terminal engine problems. That put Procter third in class in front of all the British contingents, except for an E-type Jaguar. Ken Miles in the Miles/Lew Spencer Alpine collided with an O.S.C.A. S1000 and was forced to retire. Then, with a few laps to go, Jo Sheppard in the Sheppard/Tom Payne Alpine had engine problems and pulled into the pits with a broken connecting rod and a hole in the crank case. With no chance of repair and with Sheppard out of the car and relaxing with a beer in his hand, Garrad sent him back out onto the track. Limping round, he unexpectedly managed to finish, coming in thirty-second place. The Filippo Theodoli/Freddie Barrette Harrington failed to finish due to engine problems. Procter finished fifteenth overall, third in class, settling the score from the previous year by beating all the MGs – two of which came in directly behind him. The TVR threat had faded, with their only finisher coming twenty-fifth. Rootes were able to trumpet the Alpine as the fastest car in its price class, which was quite true – although less expensive cars had finished in front of them. The Harper/Procter car was supposedly displayed at the New York Auto Show, although in reality it was Sheppard/Payne car, the Harper/Procter Alpine being too badly dented to display.

Three new Alpines were converted by Harrington for the 1962 racing season at Le Mans. In an attempt to increase airflow over the car, the front of the car kept its conventional shape but the rear had a raised Kamm tail – a flattened square rear – in effect bringing the boot lid level with the fins. The suspension was modified and weight-saving aluminium body panels fitted. With different regulations now governing the cars, the competition department were also able to uprate the engine to try and make the cars more competitive.

At the Le Mans testing session in April the Harrington body modifications proved to be effective, reducing drag by 8 per cent. Combined with the uprated engine, lap times were cut by up to 8 seconds from the previous year. However, one of the consecutively

Alpines lined up for the start of the 1962 Le Mans 24-hour race. (Chris McGovern Collection)

The Harper/Proctor Alpine passes under the Dunlop bridge. (Chris McGovern Collection)

The Hopkirk/Jopp Alpine being tailed by an Alfa Romeo Giulietta Zagato driven by Karl F. Foitek and Riccado Ricci of the Scuderia St Ambroeus team. (Chris McGovern Collection)

registered cars, 9201 RW, due to be driven by Tiny Lewis and Keith Ballisat, had proved to be rather slower than the other two. Therefore only two cars, 9202 RW and 9203 RW, would be used to compete. In the actual race, the cars again proved to be fast but forcing over 120 mph out of the small engines proved problematic. Both suffered bearing failures, possibly exacerbated by the badly sticking throttle controls causing over-revving. 9203 RW, the Paddy Hopkirk/Peter Jopp Alpine car, pulled into the pits 13.5 hours into the race with engine problems. The bearings were replaced within 45 minutes and the car was back in

Left: The Harper/Proctor Alpine gets the checkered flag. (Chris McGovern Collection)

Below: The Harper/Proctor Alpine finishes fifteenth overall. (Chris McGovern Collection)

the race, lasting another 3.5 hours before expiring completely. 9202 RW, the Peter Harper/Peter Procter Alpine, suffered the same problem and, after bearing repairs in the pits, their speed was then limited due to overdrive and gearbox problems. They finished fifteenth overall and without the silverware of the previous year – the Index of Thermal Efficiency Cup going to David Hobbs with Frank Gardener in a 1,200cc Lotus Elite. On return to Britain, 9203 RW was sold to the Alan Fraser racing team, the other two being rebuilt and retained for further use, with one appearing in the RAC Rally later that year in November.

1963 was the last year Rootes were involved with Alpines in an international racing event, after which they gave the new Sunbeam Tiger priority. At Sebring an Alpine was privately entered by American Rootes dealers Hollywood Sport Cars (sponsored by *Sports Car Graphic* magazine) and driven by Davey Jordan and Jerry Titus. The Harrington of Filippo Theodoli raced his Harrington for the second year running with Bill Kneeland and

1963 Sebring 12-hour race: Jerry Titus (left) and Davey Jordan with the Hollywood Sport Cars Alpine on the starting line with the Filippo Theodoli Harrington in the background. Jordan later raced for actor James Garner's racing team. (Davey Jordan Collection)

The Sunbeam Harrington of Filippo Theodoli finished fourth in class, thirty-sixth place overall. (Coventry Transport Museum)

Jerry Crawfod also driving. Theodoli had recently decided to modify the engine and fit non-standard Weber carburettors to improve performance for some previous SCCA circuit racing. Sharing garage space with the Ferraris of Theodoli's friend Luigi Chinetti and his North American Racing Team, it quite legitimately displayed a decal of the Ferrari prancing horse under its Alpine script badge. The Harrington was first off the start line driven by Bill Kneeland but was soon overtaken by much faster cars. After not very many laps, it pulled into the pits, short on fuel. The mechanics realised the Webers were halving normal

The Hollywood Sport Car's Alpine finished third in class, thirty-first overall. (Revs Institute of Automotive Research)

The Hollywood Sport Cars Alpine with the Ferarri 250 of Ginther and Ireland hot on their tail. (Steven Alcala)

fuel consumption on the long-distance race. In his rush to cut the officially wired seal to enable refuelling, a marshal accidently pulled out the quick-release fuel filler cap from the filler tube. Unable to get cap assembly back on and with a bodged repair using gaffer tape, the tank could only be half filled without sloshing fuel all over the track, resulting in a lot of subsequent fuel stops. It finished the slowest in its class – thirty-sixth place overall, fourth in class. However, Theodoli was delighted and broke out the champagne to celebrate, making up for the previous year's disappointing retirement. The Alpine driven by Davey Jordan and Jerry Titus finished thirty-first overall and third in class behind Porsche, despite spending an hour in the pits with a broken rear axle. However, Rootes cars did prove more resilient than the TVRs and MGs, which all retired early on.

At the 24 Hours of Le Mans race, two of the Kamm tail Alpines were entered. 9201 RW was driven by Harper and Procter and was very likely the same car that they drove the previous year, its registration number almost certainly having been swapped with its sister car some time previously. 9202 RW (previously 9201 RW) was driven by Tiny Lewis and Keith Ballisat, being the car they were scheduled to race the previous year. The team had an engine blow up in practice, the prelude to a poor showing from both cars. The Harper/Procter car blew a head gasket 6 hours into the race and retired after averaging 95 mph for ninety-three laps. The Lewis/Ballisat car was leading its class when its crankshaft broke after completing 18 hours and 200 laps, putting it out of the race as well. It was a very disappointing result, but for the following year there was the exciting possibility of greater success with the new Tiger.

The 1963 Le Mans team with the two Kamm tail Alpines. (Chris McGovern Collection)

Peter Procter during a practice session for the 1963 Le Mans 24-hour race. (Chris McGovern Collection)

Alpine 9201 RW with Peter Harper and Peter Procter in the pits during practice for the 1963 Le Mans 24-hour race. (Chris McGovern Collection)

The Harper/Procter Alpine during the 1963 Le Mans 24-hour race, in the pits before retiring with engine problems. (Chris McGovern Collection)

For Le Mans 1964, three special Tigers were built to provide publicity for the up-and-coming new production model. They were to be made with specially designed fastback bodies with the help of sports and racing car manufacturer Brian Lister. The project seemed to stall, and with no success for a year and a half Norman Garrad was unceremoniously shunted back into the sales department by the Rootes brothers. They were keen to employ Marcus Chambers, who they lured out of competition retirement from his massive successes at BMC. He took over the project, but development of the cars was too problem-stricken to be salvaged in the few months left before Le Mans. With poor untested Ford engines supplied by Shelby, as well as being overweight, with poor handling, braking and overheating problems, the untested Tigers were a disaster at Le Mans. Both of the entered cars retired with serious engine problems after running for 3 and 9 hours. The widely publicised link-up between Rootes and Chrysler had only just occurred and the planned race programme with the Tigers was immediately cancelled. Shelby had to give Rootes a refund for the poor preparation work he had done on the engines and two of the Tigers were sold off. The remaining one was given to Rootes development engineer Bernard Unett, who successfully developed and campaigned it in club racing, with impressive results in the following two seasons.

Privateers continued to enter Alpines and Tigers in some major events, including the Daytona 24-hour race in February 1966 when the Ring Free fuel company sponsored an all-ladies team of two Alpines driven by Rosemary Smith/Smokey Drolet and Suzy Dietrich Donna Mae Mims/Janet Guthrie. John Bently and John Hill also entered a Tiger. Of the fifty-nine starters, both Alpines were among the thirty-three that crossed the finishing line, in thirtieth and thirty-second place respectively, but the Bently/Hill Tiger retired with oil pressure problems. Don Bolton, Bill Buchman and Jerry Morgan's Alpine ran well in the Daytona Continental 1,000 km race, the precursor to the 24-hour event. Jerry Morgan drove the Alpine to the race, back home, and then to work the next day.

The Suzy Dietrich/Donna Mae Mims/Janet Guthrie Alpine in the 1966 Daytona 24-hour race. (Henry Ford Collection)

Club Racing

The Sunbeam Alpine was not a hugely popular choice as a club racer, but it did appear in many motor club racing events with amateur drivers in America and was also regularly seen at club events in Britain, Canada and many other countries.

North America

In North America the Sports Car Club of America (SCCA) was the sanctioning body for amateur racers from the mid-1940s. In 1962 they also began organising professional events. There were various divisions, each organising divisional events in a given geographical area to make racing competitions accessible throughout the country, and there was also a national championship. Around fifteen production car classes were based on the comparative competitive ability of the cars, using factors such as power to weight ratios, engine size and suspension. At its height there were many successful Alpine racers on the club circuits.

Vince Tamburo, a salesman from Maryland, raced an Alpine with great success in the 1960 season. Tamburo had gained experience racing an MG and a Triumph TR3 and, after a very persuasive pitch, he persuaded Rootes' sales boss in America, John Panks, to provide him with an Alpine to race. He gave Rootes their first big sports car racing success

Vince Tamburo, America's G production champion in 1960. (Vince Tamburo Jnr)

when he won the 1960 G Production Class National Championship. Tamburo had four outright wins and three second places out of a series of nine races. This proved that, for a relatively small outlay, the Alpine could beat the more expensive cars in its class. The

Vince Tamburo's G Production Class Alpine (centre) on the grid at Cumberland Speedway, Maryland, 1960. (Vince Tamburo Jnr)

Vince Tamburo, pictured here in a loaned, poorly prepared F Production Class Alpine in 1962, this probably being his last race in an Alpine. (Steve Silverstein)

limited modifications allowed in G Production Class worked to the advantage of the Alpine because, as a relatively unmodified car, it had better brakes and superior handling than most of its rivals such as the Deutsch-Bonnet, Fiat-Arbath 850 and Porsche 1300. It was heavier, but did have a comparatively higher engine capacity. The allowed engine modifications were limited to balancing, polishing of combustion chambers and cleaning of the ports. Limited modification of camshaft and suspension was permitted, otherwise it was down to a choice of tyres and shock absorbers. Rootes regarded publicity from such successes as very important in increasing sales, so, like BMC and Standard Triumph, they began to regularly sponsor club racers who were also sometimes Rootes dealers themselves. By the 1963 season Rootes were paying prize money for a first, second or third placed Alpine regardless of overall position, and double if you won a race. The competitors were quite likely to make money, which could amount thousands of dollars in today's terms. Rootes, as with Tamburo, would sometimes provide a car. Bob Grossman and then Jim Latimer raced one factory supplied Series III in the north-east, and Ken Miles another on the west coast.

Bud Rose, a Rootes dealer in Walnut Creek, California, was one of the dealers to take up the Rootes offer of financial and technical assistance to race the new Series II Alpine, which had been reclassified in F Production Class for the 1961 season. Rootes wanted to continue to raise the profile of the car, which, despite Tamburo's efforts, was acquiring the nickname 'The British Thunderbird'. This was far from complimentary, the Thunderbird being in no way a sports car. *Sports Car Graphic* magazine had described it as a rapid, easy-to-drive street machine, but unlikely to lure anyone into a crash hat. Rootes sent Rose a new Series II engine and all the new Rootes tuning kits to upgrade a Series I. They were fitted by Sherman Allen, who thought that on paper the improvements looked fairly insignificant. Actual results were dramatic, increasing horsepower by 14 per cent, with Allen then raising it considerably more with some of his own tuning tricks. Racing driver Steve Froines was

Rootes originally supplied this Series III to Bob Grossman to race in the 1963 season. Pictured is Jim Latimer (on a very wet track at Mid-Ohio Sports Car Course), who purchased the car to race in the 1964 season. (John McCollister Collection)

competing in his own Alfa 1300 but it was getting rather too expensive for him to race, so with some reservations he accepted Bud Rose's job offer to pilot the Alpine, not expecting great results. However, *Sports Car Graphic* were soon having to take back their comments, now calling the Series II a ferocious racing machine with not only need of a crash hat, but a trophy shelf as well. The Bud Rose Alpine, nicknamed *Rosebud*, had considerable success in local SCCA events. Froines took four first place finishes in *Rosebud*'s first season before it was lent to Rootes for Jack Brabham and Stirling Moss to drive in the 1961 Riverside 3-hour endurance race. Froines went on to successfully pilot other Alpines, one originally prepared from various competition leftovers for Bob Richman by Doane Spencer at Cal Autos in San Francisco. It was so quick it was impounded by stewards after one race for suspected rule infringements for a win, beating a Porsche 356.

Don Sesslar from Columbus, Ohio, started racing an Alpine in late 1960. After competing in stock car racing, his sports car racing career began in 1957 with a Porsche Spyder, finishing twelfth in the Sports Car Club of America Championship points table. He won his first national championship in 1959 driving a Porsche RSK in the F modified class and also won the prestigious Sports Car Club of America Presidents' Cup. The Alpine Sesslar raced was campaigned by Sports Car Forum, a Rootes dealer in Columbus. It was run by H. J. Meyer, the president of the dealership, with Claude Gaines as vice president and with mechanic Shorty Bickel. Although only really testing out the Alpine in the first season, Sesslar had several first place finishes. In 1961 the same Alpine was uprated by fitting a Series II engine and more modifications, and took Sesslar to second place in the national rankings. Sesslar described the Alpine as one of the finest handling cars he had driven with superb braking, often allowing him to beat Porsches by out-braking them and overtaking on the inside of a corner. Lack of limited slip differential and widely spaced lower gears was a disadvantage, so the Alpine tended to do better on the faster tracks where it could keep up momentum.

Sesslar finished in third place in the national rankings in 1962 driving the Series II. For 1963 only, the Alpine was classified in the tougher E Production Class, racing against cars such as the

Steve Froines in Cal Autos' F Production Class Alpine at Candlestick race track in 1965, where he had a class win. The fins were cut down to Series IV style after Froines damaged the rear end spinning the back end into a fence post. (Revs Institute of Automotive Research)

Austin Healey 100/4, and the Porsche 356. According to Sesslar, there was considerable support from Rootes. Driver Norman Lamb won the SCCA Southwest Division Championship in an Alpine and Sesslar managed to tie in the points table with Lake Underwood's Porsche 356 in the national championship. However with more overall first places, Underwood became the official national champion. At Thompson Speedway Motorsports Park in the eleventh round, Sesslar missed a fifth place and some points by half a car length. Fifth place would have secured him the extra points needed to eventually win the championship. In 1964 Don Sesslar drove a new Series IV Alpine and finally had an outright win in the National F Production Class National Championship, with five race wins and two second places in a series of eleven races. A national advertising campaign featuring the car was instigated by a delighted Rootes, helping to give the best year ever for Sunbeam sales in America.

Don Sesslar preparing for a victory lap in the Sports Car Forum Series I Alpine in 1962. He took a class win, battling it out with Skip Barber's Turner Alexander at the Bridgehampton race track. (H. J. Myer Collection)

Don Sesslar on his way to a class win at Mid-Ohio Sports Car Course in the Sports Car Forum Series IV Alpine in 1964. He would secure his victory in the National Championship F Production Class at Watkins Glen in August. (H. J. Myers Collection)

Dan Carmichael, a Columbus architect, raced the same Sports Car Forum Alpine Series IV from 1964 to 1967. Carmichael shared the use of the car with Sesslar, winning the 1964 Central Divisional Championship. In 1965 Carmichael again won the Central Divisional Championship, this time also officially counting as a national Championship because of a change in the scoring system. The introduction of the Tiger brought cash-strapped Rootes into competition with the big bore cars in B Production, and the well-supported works teams that ran cars such as the Ford Mustang, Chevrolet Corvettes and Jaguars. Rootes contracted Carol Shelby to build four race-prepared Tigers. Lew Spencer had the honour of winning the Tiger's first competition honours in the Pacific Coast Divisional Championship, creating lots of publicity. He won the B Production event at an average speed of 89 mph, finishing 12 seconds ahead of the second placed Jaguar XKE. Only this first 'development' Tiger was completed by Shelby before Rootes pulled out of the arrangement, giving the Tiger to Sports Car Forum in September 1964.

Both Don Sesslar and Dan Carmichael raced this Tiger, Carmichael qualifying in it for the first American Road Race of Champions held in November at Riverside. Carmichael used a west coast supplied Tiger in the same event, finishing fourth or fifth in B production. At Nassau the Shelby Tiger was badly damaged when Sesslar spun trying to avoid a Lotus. For the 1965 season Sports Car Forum built a new Tiger by putting the remnants of the Shelby development Tiger into a new body shell. Sessler raced it in about a dozen events, while Carmichael competed in the Alpine. 1965 saw both Carmichael and Sesslar round off a successful year

First victory for the Tiger in SCCA competition, with Lew Spencer driving the Shelby Tiger in the West Coast Divisional Championship. Spencer won the B Production Class event, finishing 12 seconds ahead of the second-placed car, a Jaguar XKE. (Coventry Transport Museum)

The Shelby development Tiger (foreground) next to the Alpine in the paddock at Greenwood Roadway in 1964. Jim Latimer's Series III is in the background. (John McCollister Collection)

The Shelby development Tiger car with Ken Miles in the paddock at the Road America 500 meeting at Elkhart Lake in 1964, where he finished first in B Production Class. Miles was to co-drive the car with Don Sesslar, but Sesslar broke some ribs racing another car so could not take part. (John McCollister Collection)

by competing in the American Road Race of Champions at Daytona. Unfortunately, both cars were hit by other competitors' cars during their class races, putting both of them out of contention for the title. At some point a new 1,725cc engine was installed in the Alpine, but by then the dealership was sold, thus ending local support. The Tiger was sold and Sesslar moved into Trans-Am racing. Carmichael himself financed what would be his last season racing the Alpine. He came third in the 1967 Central Division Championship and finished in second place to Bob Sharp (racing teammate of film star Paul Newman) in a Datsun 1600 at the American Road Race of Champions at Daytona. Datsun really wanted a championship win and sent their cars to Daytona weeks in advance of the race. They rented a tuning workshop where factory mechanics set up the cars for the drivers, thus providing exceptionally tough competition.

Testing the Sports Car Forum Alpine and new Tiger at Mid-Ohio, May 1965. From left to right: Dan Carmichael, mechanic Shorty Bickel, Don Sesslar and Claude Gains. (John McCollister Collection)

Dan Carmichael at the 1965 American Road Race Championship. (Steve Silverstein Collection)

American Road Race of Champions, 1967, where Dan Carmichael took the Alpine to second place in the championship. (John McCollister Collection)

West coast Rootes dealership Hollywood Sport Cars of California was owned by Chic Vandergriff. He sponsored many of the racing cars competing in the area and had connections with racing driver Jerry Titus, then editor of *Sports Car Graphic* magazine. Titus often featured 'project' cars in articles, one in particular being 'Project Alpine' that followed the preparation of the Hollywood Sport Cars Alpine for the events in which it took part, such as the Sebring 12 hours and the Riverside Grand Prix. After racing the Hollywood Sport Cars Alpine at Sebring in 1963, racing driver Davey Jordan continued to drive the Alpine during the following season. With mechanical problems and tough competition from the Austin Healey 3000 and MGB, results were not brilliant. With assistance from Rootes drying up as their financial situation worsened, the Hollywood Alpine did not compete the following year.

From 1967 onwards there were rule changes allowing greater modifications to both suspension and engines for production racing cars, lessening the Alpine's natural advantages. The engine was also already pretty much tuned to the limit. With the financial problems at Rootes, the new Tiger and Imp started to take priority, reducing the technical and financial assistance that Rootes gave to dealers for racing Alpines. When Chrysler took over, the support for club racers suffered even more. With lack of support and with the new five bearing 1,725cc engine initially proving less suitable for racing, by 1967 regular appearances of Alpines on the American race track were far fewer.

One of the last active Alpines in SCCA events was that of the Visalia Dodge Boys, which was raced by Tom Elliot and Skip Adrian. Adrian had previously built and raced a Sunbeam Rapier with repair shop owner and ex-Hollywood Sport Cars mechanic Bob Hagin in 1965 and 1966. Elliot owned a Dodge dealership in Visalia, California and was known for racing speed boats but wanted to move into sports car racing. He began attending racing drivers' school, meeting Adrian who was working there as a racing instructor. They decided to obtain and race a red Series V Alpine. Throughout 1967 and 1968 Adrian competed in national events and Elliot raced in divisional events, sharing the car and visiting most of the tracks on the west coast. Although SCCA classifications had moved more competitive and lighter cars into the Alpine's group, they were successful enough for Rootes to offer them sponsorship for the 1969 season, but they turned down the offer to move into Formula cars with sponsorship from Visalia Dodge.

Britain and Ireland

British Rootes stalwart Alan Fraser's very first competitive event was the Alpine Rally in 1952, where he drove with distinction finishing fourth in class. The following year he started his motoring business in Kent, later becoming a Rootes dealer and competing regularly in the Monte Carlo Rally in Sunbeam Rapiers. He began to build a racing team in the early sixties, often appearing at Goodwood with Rapiers, then Alpines. He regularly entered his red Sunbeam Harrington Le Mans, registered MEL 63, the ex-works Le Mans Alpine 9203 RW and sometimes the factory-owned car 9201 RW in various races and rallies. Records are sketchy, but it is known that all three cars took part in the 1962 Tourist Trophy at Goodwood, but with only Peter Harper finishing with 9201 RW in twelfth place. MEL 63 took part in the Veedol Trophy series later the same year, during which it was badly damaged crashing in a race at Goodwood. It was again damaged when crashing later in the year on the RAC

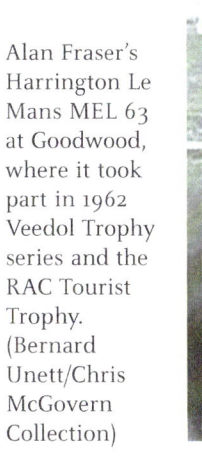

Alan Fraser's Harrington Le Mans MEL 63 at Goodwood, where it took part in 1962 Veedol Trophy series and the RAC Tourist Trophy. (Bernard Unett/Chris McGovern Collection)

75

Rally, but continued to make appearances for Fraser for some time. Fraser later campaigned his own personal transport, a Sunbeam Tiger, and also a car nicknamed the 'Monster' Tiger. Built by Bernard Unett, it was very competitive, winning many races outright and finishing first in class, second overall in the Fred Dixon Marque Trophy. Fraser is best known for his great success with his Hillman Imp racing team in the mid-1960s with drivers such as Unett, Nick Britten, Peter Harper, Jacqui Smith and Ray Calcutt. In a Rootes-backed project, he also developed what must have been the ultimate Hillman Imp based car, a GT racer, with designer Tom Killeen. Known as the Fraser GT, it was built with the intention of competing in the 24 Hours of Le Mans in 1967, but the merger of Rootes with Chrysler scuppered the project and it only got as far as the initial testing stage.

Bernard Unett, who, as a Rootes development engineer, worked on the Sunbeam Alpine development programme in Coventry, started racing an Alpine in 1961. Encouraged by Mike Parkes of the competition department, Unett bought from the factory one of the eight original pre-production prototypes to prepare for racing. Registered XRW 302, It had been used as a 'model' car in the design department and so had escaped the worst rigors of development testing. Although sent home by the stewards for his terrible driving at his first race meeting, his technique quickly improved. Unett developed the car for racing by uprating the suspension and increasing engine power with modifications, including a bespoke racing camshaft specially manufactured in Sweden, making the car very quick. As in America, the Alpine was initially rather underrated as a racing car in Britain, but, unlike its American counterparts, it never really caught on with British racers and comparatively few were seen on the race track. However, with its good handling and superior braking, Unett turned the Alpine into a very competitive racer. Various British clubs such as the British Automobile Racing Club arranged national events and 1962 saw Unett take part in the BARC Veedol Motor Racing Competition, a series to encourage novice racers sponsored by J. Paul Getty's oil company. Unett did reasonably well, getting as far as the final, which was the support race at the Tourist Trophy meeting at the Goodwood race circuit. Mr Getty himself presented the Veedol Cup to winner Bob Burnard with his AC Bristol.

Continuing to race the Alpine regularly and gaining experience, Unett entered the Freddie Dixon Challenge Trophy in 1964, a series open to specified marques and one of the big prizes in British club racing at the time. In the second of eleven races, Unett raced against up-and-coming driver Jackie Stewart, Stewart's car breaking down on the third lap at the Oulton Park circuit. Although missing out on the next race and his engine blowing up in practice before another, Unett eventually came through to an overall championship victory, winning by one point and beating his main rival John Sharp and his MGB in an exciting final at the Aintree International circuit. Unett had also regularly beaten off such cars as the TVR Grantura, Elva Courier, Triumph TR3, Morgan and several Austin Healey 3000s. This was quite an achievement, even more so than it would have been in previous years. With the increasing popularity of club racing, competition was getting fierce and one would have to be a competent driver in a really good car to stand a chance of success in any race.

Marcus Chambers, now the Rootes competition department manager, gave Unett one of the Lister-built Tigers to campaign in the 1965 season. Registered ADU 180B, it was one of the two that had embarrassingly short outings at the Le Mans 24-hour race the year before. Working on the car, which was stored in a chicken coup on his parents' farm, Unett transformed it into a reliable racer and fell just short of major championship wins,

Bernard Unett with pre-production prototype Alpine XRW 302 in a 1964 Nottingham Sports Car Club event at the Silverstone circuit. (Bernard Unett/Chris McGovern Collection)

The start of round nine of the 1964 Freddie Dixon Challenge Trophy marque race at Goodwood, organized by the British Automobile Racing Club. In third place is the MGB of D. C. Milner, getting squeezed between Bernard Unett in XRW 302 and Tommy Entwistle leading in his TVR Grantura. (Bernard Unett)

Charles Eyre-Maunsell in the final of the 1962 Irish Sports Car Championship. (Chris McGovern Collection)

coming a very close second in the Autosport Championship in 1965 and 1966. Unett also raced very successfully in the Fraser racing team, particularly with the Hillman Imp, then later became British touring car champion three times in the Hillman Avenger during the seventies. He was also development engineer, test driver and roadside support for the World Rally Championship-winning Chrysler and Peugeot teams managed by Des O'Dell.

Charles Eyre-Maunsell was well known in Ireland for taking part in many rallies, but he also successfully competed in sports car racing in Sunbeam Alpines. He won the 1962 and 1963 Irish Sports Car Championship.

Canada

John Antons, Eppie Wietzes and Dennis Coad all raced Sunbeam Alpines successfully in Canadian club events in the early 1960s. Antons started racing in an Austin Healey Sprite in American events in 1959, graduating to a Porsche 356 for 1960 and 1961. He then raced a fast Sunbeam Alpine very successfully in the 1962 season both in Canadian and American events, gaining many first and second places before moving on to a Lotus Mark VI in 1963. Eppie Wietzes, originally from the Netherlands, ran a Rootes dealership, service and repair business and began racing with a Morris Minor. His mechanic Paul Cooke talked Rootes into giving them a Series II Alpine to campaign. They placed an order for a top spec model, then sold the extras such as the wire wheels, radio and hard top to help finance their first

John Antons in May 1962 at the Westwood Motor Circuit, Vancouver. (Chris McGovern Collection)

Eppie Wietzes in his Alpine at the Mosport Park racetrack, near Boumanville, Ontario. (Wietzes Family)

year's racing. After successfully racing the Alpine, Wietzes eventually sold it to Diana Carter who raced it for one season.

It was then passed to George Eaton of the famed Eaton department store chain, who also raced it before graduating to a 427 Shelby Cobra. Dennis Coad raced a Rootes Inc. Canada works Series II Alpine as number 200, which was very successful in club events. It had dozens of engine modifications and was lightened by stripping the body and interior, removing items such as headlights and any superfluous bodywork including the boot floor and door supports. Craig Fisher and Ian Hart later raced the car. Hart worked for the Channel Nine TV station, so the car's racing number was then changed to number 9. With the introduction of the Series IV, Rootes reshaped the back end of the car with cut-down fins and later replaced the engine with the 1,725cc version. The car continued to have success in club events up to as late as 1975.

The Dennis Coad Alpine shown here was later raced by Craig Fisher and Ian Hart. Records are poor, but this picture of a victory lap could well be documenting that of Diana Carter, who owned and raced the Eppie Wietzes Alpine. (Craig Fisher Collection, courtesy of Mike Nilson)

Alpines battle for position at Harewood Acres. Both cars are now owned by Alan Weller. (Craig Fisher Collection, courtesy of Mike Nilson)

Dennis Coad raced the Canadian works Alpine as number 200. Eventually, the fins were clipped and a 1,725cc engine installed for Ian Hart to race as Number 9. (Alan Weller)

Publicity photo taken at the Rootes Canada head office in 1966, with Rootes rally team member Rosemary Smith posing next to ex-Coad, now the number 9, Ian Hart Alpine. (Alan Weller)

Ownership

There is a certain joy in owning a classic car. It is not so much about performance, but how it makes you feel. Enjoying your car is what it's all about. Although in its standard form the Sunbeam Alpine is not the quickest of classic 1960s sports cars, it will definitely put a smile on your face when you take it motoring – and in a classic car like the Alpine, you are motoring, a far more all-encompassing and satisfying venture than simply driving.

The Sunbeam Alpine is a much nicer daily driver than its contemporaries such as the MGB and the Triumph TR3. It has a good driving position with a stylish, roomy interior and comfortable seats. The soft top is adequately watertight and the hard-top makes a great winter option. It is still able to keep up with modern traffic and with overdrive fitted it will cruise comfortably on the motorway. There is a tendency for some Alpines to overheat when stationary in traffic for some time, so it is not uncommon for an electric cooling fan to be added. Despite the Hillman Husky-based platform, the ride is supple, the cruciform is very effective at preventing body flexing and in its day the handling and road holding was good enough to make it a top club racer. Steering is light and the gear change smooth and slick but full synchromesh is only on cars from late 1964 onwards. With its pretty 1960s styling, the Series V probably makes the best classic daily driver with its more powerful five bearing 1,725cc engine, more sophisticated suspension, alternator and more luxurious ride. For purity of line, with the fins and original rounded top of the 1950s-styled original, but also with slight improvements, the Series II makes a really nice weekend car (although you will have to put up with the smaller capacity boot).

Rust is the biggest concern that buyers need to consider. There are many potential places for the underside and body to corrode. The complex three-layer sills are crucial to the car's strength, and a severely corroded car will literally fold in the middle when jacked up from the rear jacking points with the tool kit jack. If the doors open and shut properly with up to 2 mm movement in the door panel gap when jacked up, the car should be reasonably solid. If they don't, then as well as rotten sills, rust may be in the ends of the cruciform structure or the front mountings of the rear springs. On level ground the car should sit level if springs and shocks have not deteriorated. Badly fitting doors could indicate hinge mount problems, rotting bulkhead, or the car beginning to fold due to rotten sills. The joins between the floor and the front and rear body sections are also a rust trap, especially at the front when sealant erodes. Being a stronger joint, they are sometimes badly repaired using filler alone, which can be revealed by use of a magnet. Photographic evidence of sill repairs in progress is the only

A sister car to the 1954 Stirling Moss winning Alpine at the Goodwood Revival. An argument between driver Peter Collins and co-driver Ronnie Adams led to disqualification on the 1953 Alpine Rally. In the 1954 Alpine Rally, Collins and co-driver Lewis Garrad suffered a broken differential and the car was forced to retire. (John Willshire)

A Sunbeam Venezia on display at a vintage car show in Belgium. (Paul Vanrusselt)

Mick Sullivan's Series IV Alpine *Stitch*, which he bought in 1981 for £130 and then used as a daily driver for four years. After a full refurbishment Mick now uses *Stitch* on high days and holidays. (Mick Sullivan)

Rear view of Derek Hewitson's Series C Harrington Alpine, showing the rear hatch. (Derek Hewitson)

way to be sure they have been done properly. On Ryton factory cars, dimples in front of the windscreen indicate this twin-skinned section is being forced apart by rust. The inside of the wheel arches can rot and let water into the sill structure, and the Series III to V windscreen frames can rot badly at the bottom. Rot along the bottom edge of doors is common if drainage holes are blocked. Series I and II hard tops are aluminium so don't normally corrode but can suffer from cracking, while the later steel hard tops are more prone to rust.

Alpines are mechanically simple and engines are solid and reliable if properly maintained. Clattery engines can be due to worn cam followers, and valve guide wear can cause engines to smoke. Oil leaks from the engine through the oil seals, often collecting on the spark plug recesses, are very common but there is a modern fix. Transmissions are rugged and simple, as is the running gear. With good owners' club support, commonality of components with the Hillman Humber and Singer and several specialist parts suppliers, there is good provision for spare parts. The mechanicals are simple enough for DIY repairs and maintenance, otherwise your average local garage should be able to cope.

If you are not concerned about keeping your car as original as possible there is plenty of scope for modifications which can dramatically increase the performance for road use or competition. Rootes made two stages of special engine tuning available on the introduction of the 80-bhp-engined Series II Alpine, which included camshaft, flywheel, engine oil cooler, brake, axle and suspension kits. Many carburettor conversion kits were also available and American racers of the 1960s achieved around 100 bhp, with about 83 hp getting to the rear wheels, using such modifications. Specialists such as Chris Draycot's Sunbeam Classic Spares now offer upgrades of up to 185 bhp. Chris himself races a very quick Series V.

There are various options for attempting to improve performance by changing the original carburettor setups, but without doubt the best carburation solution for road-going Alpines is now the newly available Alpine manifold/Weber carburettor kit. First envisaged by Eddie Zetlein, the new manifold was developed by Eddie, Jerome Senn, Peter Pescud and other key members of the Sunbeam Alpine Owners' Club with Webcon UK Ltd. It is a development and amalgamation of an old Mangoletsi design used for the Hillman Hunter and a manifold that was sourced from New Zealand some years ago by Carl Christiansen for his American ex-factory Alpine race car he used in classic racing on the west coast. The new manifold's much improved shape allows a very significant improvement in fuel distribution and employs a custom re-jetted version of the Weber 32/36 carburettor. Compared with the Rootes setup of the original standard manifold with twin Stromberg carbs, it has shown in tests to provide a more than 17 per cent improvement in power and torque.

Another option is to transplant an engine. A choice often considered is the Holbay H120, a highly tuned version of the original Series V 1,725cc engine, which in various specifications can give up to around 120 bhp. It was developed by Holbay for the Sunbeam Rapier fastback launched in October 1968 and also used in the Hillman Hunter GLS unveiled in 1972. A slightly de-tuned version was used for road cars, which was more acceptable for everyday use compared to the original unfettered version, both of which are now sometimes used for competition. The Holbay engine often sports a pair of Weber 40 DCOE carburettors. They look and sound great, but are difficult to fit because of the long, tilted manifold.

Some opt for the more radical choice of a modern engine. Bill Ashby who lives in Colorado was dissatisfied with the already modified Alpine he had bought. He stripped everything out and started again. Bill designed over 100 custom brackets, assemblies and parts to install a turbo-charged Nissan CA18DET twin-cam 1,850cc engine, delivering 238 hp to the rear wheels, along with an aluminium radiator, five-speed Nissan gearbox and a custom stainless steel dual exhaust system. These are all part of a long list that would take up a whole page. The body was soda stripped and resprayed a stunning shade of blue, the plush refurbished interior getting retro leather Mazda Miata heated sports seats with four-point safety harnesses, a dual hoop bolt-in roll bar and Moto-lita 14-inch steering wheel. A modern Ford Zetec or a Toyota V6 are among other engines that will also fit.

There are ample Alpine and Rootes related owners' clubs who aim to bring members together to provide information and preservation of the Alpine and other Rootes marques and to further encourage interest in motoring and motorsport. Regular meetings are

Bill Ashby was dissatisfied with the modified Alpine he had bought, so stripped everything out to fit a twin-cam turbo-charged Nissan engine. Bodywork and interior were also completely re-done. (Curtis Jacobson)

85

Bill Ashby's 1,850cc turbo-charged, twin-cam Nissan five-speed engine delivers 238 hp to the rear wheels of his modified Alpine. (Curtis Jacobson)

Alpines line up outside the Coventry Transport Museum on a SAOC day trip. (David Bradley)

usually organised so members can meet and drive their cars or compete in concourse, driving, or racing and rally competitions. 2009 was a big year for Alpine owners' clubs, being the fiftieth anniversary of the 'Series' Sunbeam Alpine marque. There was recognition at a special SAOC display at the Silverstone Classic Meeting, where the chief Alpine development engineer, Don Tarbun, and prototype test driver Mike Adlington were reunited with notable Alpines such as the Le Mans winner and the only surviving factory prototype. The SOAC also arranged a fiftieth-anniversary rally with fifty or so Alpines from Europe all meeting for celebrations on the French Riviera at Cannes, the original location for the unveiling of the Alpine in 1959. The Grand Hotel hosted a champagne reception for owners and guests with dozens of Alpines lined up on the front lawns of the hotel after a seafront procession along the Boulevard de la Croisette.

The Index of Thermal Efficiency Le Mans winner at the Silverstone Classic Meeting fiftieth anniversary display. It was restored by Justin Harrington in the early 1990s. (John Willshire)

Special guest – chief Alpine development engineer Don Tarbun – with SAOC members, inspecting Cindy and Paul Carlton's Series II Alpine at the fiftieth anniversary display at the 2009 Silverstone Classic Meeting. From left to right: Don Tarbun, Rod Wallis, Cindy Carlton and Jacqui Tarbun. (John Willshire)

A standard engine, that of Chas Mangion's Series II Alpine. Rootes had increased its capacity to 1,600cc from the 1,500cc of the Series I engine. (Chas Mangion)

87

Alpines on the lawn of the Grand Hotel in Cannes during the Sunbeam Alpine Owners' Club fiftieth anniversary rally. (David Bradley)

Guests at the champagne reception at the Grand Hotel in Cannes, celebrating fifty years of the 'Series' Sunbeam Alpine marque. (David Bradley)

SAOC members Bob and Marie standing in their Series V Alpine on the fiftieth anniversary rally, leaving the Le Provençal Golf Club after lunch. (John Willshire)

For owners who want even more excitement, a track day will give you a chance to drive to the limit and get the best out of your car in a safe and controlled environment. Provided by most racing circuits around the world, instructors are usually available for individual advice and tuition. Tyres will need a decent amount of tread, brakes will need to be in good condition (a change of brake fluid is advisable) and engine oil/water levels need checking throughout the day along with filters and hoses before you start. Steering and wheel bearings should be free of excessive play and you will need a suitable helmet. It is recommended to have towing eyes fitted in case your car breaks down, otherwise marshals will attach tow straps as best they can to wherever they can.

Speed events is the name given to speed hill climbing and sprinting on tarmac and must be one of the best ways to get your Alpine into motor sport. It's you against the clock in a branch of motor sport which has a great atmosphere and welcomes newcomers. In Britain events take place on private roads or tracks nearly every weekend between April and October, organised by the Climb and Sprint Association, but sprinting on the flat is not generally recognised outside the UK. Most European countries have hill climbing competitions which tend to be of greater length and on public roads. Hill climbing is also popular in North America (Pikes Peak and Mount Washington being examples) and Australia. UK-based Alpine owner Mike Broome competes in the handicapped class where your target time is based on your previous best time or practice time at that venue, so everyone has a chance of a good result. Mike began by attending one of the many hill climb schools using his company car, then

The Visalia Dodge Boys Alpine on the Mount Washington hill climb. (Dan Houde/Mt Washington Auto Road photo library)

89

graduated to compete regularly in his extensively modified Holbay-engined Series V Alpine. His competition successes in his Alpine include first and second in class at the Goodwood Circuit Sprint, three wins and a second in class at the Shelsley Walsh Hill Climb and two wins, three seconds and a third in class at the Prescott Hill Climb. The Bugatti owners' club currently runs an excellent handicapped class for historic cars such as the Alpine.

A classic car tour with a group of like-minded classic car owners can be an excellent way to enjoy using your car and meet other enthusiasts in a relaxed environment. Such tours are arranged by many clubs and organisations. Rallying for classic cars can be divided into different types and levels of difficulty. In Britain rallies are run by various clubs and vary from single day, weekend, night and marathon events. The two popular types for classic cars are regularity and special tests, and are usually a combination of both. The regularity

Mike Broome in his Holbay-engined series V Alpine at the 2013 May Bank Holiday Sprint meeting at Crystal Palace. (Mike Lambert, Gridshot Photography)

Matt Ollman in his Series V with Peter Gal on the 2012 Harvest Tour, organised by the Historic Rally Car Register. (tonylarge.net)

sections take place on public roads where you drive at a quite low pre-determined average speed between two or more points. More difficult rallies can involve a change of average target speeds throughout, secret time checks and challenging navigation exercises. The special tests can be on tarmac, gravel or both and involve manoeuvring between obstacles against the clock on private land or closed roads. You need a navigator and some timing equipment that can range from an ordinary stopwatch to a dashboard-mounted digital timer, trip meter and clock. In Britain, for some rallies drivers and navigators will require a non-race competition licence. Peter Kleyn first rallied his Series V Sunbeam Alpine in 2005 when he was invited to enter a Monte-style charity event from London to Monaco. Surprised at finishing ninth overall and being the highest placed UK finisher, he got the rally bug and continued to regularly enter events organised by the Historic Rally Car Register. Peter has now racked up eighteen trophies in forty championship rallies and is edging towards competing in the top Experts Class. In general, classic rally cars are not extensively modified. Peter's car has two twin-choke Weber carburettors and a Holbay-style cylinder head along with a sumpguard, stiffened suspension and rally seats.

Classic and historic circuit racing can range from small club meetings to big events like the Goodwood Revival, the Silverstone Classic meeting and the Le Mans Classic, all of which have seen recent appearances by Alpines and Tigers. Harington Le Mans owner Glenn Brackenbridge has competed several times in the Sunbeam Challenge, a circuit racing event for Alpine and Tiger owners. Glenn has a National B competition

Navigator Gaius Hiscox and Peter Kleyn driving his Series V Alpine, competing in the Hughes Rally organized by the Blackpalfrey Motor Club of Kent. (Andrew Manston, M&H Photography)

licence and is developing his 1961 Harrington for track racing. It has a full roll cage, a fire extinguisher system, an external engine cut off and other safety devices as per the rules in the Motor Sports Association 'blue book'. He has also participated in the Prescott Hill Climb, Goodwood and Brooklands events and several tours. The car was prepared for classic rallying by its previous owner Tony Barron and has an impressive record in a dozen major classic club rally events.

The Don Sesslar/Dan Carmichael F Production Championship-winning Alpine is now owned by Steve Silverstein who, after seeing an advertisement, bought the car to use for spares. After finding old receipts for performance parts, he uncovered its significant racing history and decided to refurbish the Alpine rather than totally restore it. The body was quite sound after thirty years of indoor storage, the only real damage being

Glenn Brackenridge's Sunbeam Harrington Le Mans in the paddock at the Goodwood Circuit. (Glenn Brackenridge)

Glenn Brackenridge's Sunbeam Harrington Le Mans at Donington Park Racing Circuit, leading the Lister Sunbeam Tiger of Tony Eckford in the 2014 Sunbeam Challenge. (David Davenall)

Steve Silverstein with Don Sesslar sitting at the wheel of his 1964 National Championship-winning Alpine when reunited with the car in 2005. It covered over 2,400 miles in competition without failing to finish, with Dan Carmichael also racing it. (Steve Silverstein)

The Alpine Payne and Sheppard drove in the 1962 Sebring 12-hour race, subsequently given to Rootes dealer Len Amato on condition he raced it in the north-east of the US to promote the Sunbeam Owners' Club. It was discovered as something of a wreck by Steve Silverstein in 2002 and fully restored to racing condition by Stephen Alcala. (Gerry Swetsky)

on the front right wing where it had collided with another Alpine in the American Road Race of Champions. Steve has used the Alpine to compete in Eastern vintage sports car events and the Lime Rock Vintage Fall Festival and recently won the Vintage class in the Mount Washington Hill Climb. His extensive Alpine research has uncovered several other significant racers, including the Sheppard/Payne Sebring car which has been subsequently restored by Steven Alcala.

Other restored Alpines with racing history include the sole surviving factory prototype XRW 302, restored by Simon Goldby, which I now have the privilege of owning. Simon used the car every day for some years then put it into storage. On discovering its history, he began a five-year restoration project in 1995. It has recently made appearances on the track and in displays at the Goodwood Revival and the Silverstone Classic, and was runner up in the *Practical Classics* magazine's 'Classic Car of the Year'. The Harrington Le Mans Thermal

The author on the left with *Classic Car* magazine's Phil Bell and pre-production prototype Alpine XRW 302 on the 2013 'Classic Car of the Year' stand at the National Exhibition Center, Birmingham, where it was runner-up. (David Willshire)

ADU 180B, the Le Mans Lister Tiger which was modified and successfully raced by Bernard Unett in the 1965 and 1966 seasons in Britain. It now takes part in American club racing events. (John McCollister Collection)

The ex-Le Mans racer 9201 RW on the Croft Race Circuit in 2009. (Ian Hardy)

Efficiency Cup winner 3000 RW, Le Mans Alpine 9203 RW, along with Le Mans Alpines 3001 RW and 9201 RW, have also been restored and have all appeared at major events such as the Le Mans Classic meeting and the Goodwood Revival. The Lister Tigers and the Sports Car Forum Tiger also survive and currently take part in classic racing.

Bibliography

Langworth, Richard, *Tiger, Alpine, Rapier* (1982).
McGovern, Chris, *Alpine: The Classic Sunbeam* (1980).
Robson, Graham, *Sunbeam Alpine Tiger: The Complete Story* (1996).

My thanks to Steve Silverstein for lending his extensive knowledge of American racing Alpines, to Ian and Jan at www.haringtonalpine.org for guidance on Harrington facts and figures and to Alan Weller for Canadian racing information..

The author's Series V Alpine, which was manufactured within the last six months of production. (Richard Moore)